THE *EX* Boyfriend BOOK

To Write to the Author

If you wish to contact the author or would like more information about this book, please write to the author in care of Llewellyn Worldwide and we will forward your request. Both the author and publisher appreciate hearing from you and learning of your enjoyment of this book and how it has helped you. Llewellyn Worldwide cannot guarantee that every letter written to the author can be answered, but all will be forwarded. Please write to:

Rowan Davis
℅ Llewellyn Worldwide
2143 Wooddale Drive, Dept. 978-0-7387-1143-0
Woodbury, MN 55125-2989, U.S.A.

Please enclose a self-addressed stamped envelope for reply,
or $1.00 to cover costs. If outside U.S.A., enclose
international postal reply coupon.

Many of Llewellyn's authors have websites with additional information and resources. For more information, please visit our website at http://www.llewellyn.com.

A *Zodiac* Guide to *Your Former Flames*

THE *Ex* Boyfriend BOOK

ROWAN DAVIS

Llewellyn Publications
Woodbury, Minnesota

First Edition
First Printing, 2008

Book design and format by Donna Burch
Cover art © 2007 Kun-Sung Chung
Cover design by Ellen Dahl
Edited by Andrea Neff
Llewellyn is a registered trademark of Llewellyn Worldwide, Ltd.

Library of Congress Cataloging-in-Publication Data
Davis, Rowan.
        The ex-boyfriend book : a zodiac guide to your former flames / Rowan
            Davis.—1st ed.
            p. cm.
        ISBN 978-0-7387-1143-0
        1. Astrology. 2. Love—Miscellanea. 3. Single men—Psychology—
        Miscellanea. 4. Man-woman relationships—Miscellanea.
        5. Separation (Psychology)—Miscellanea. I. Title.

    BF1729.L6D37 2007
    133.5'864677—dc22   2007037081

Llewellyn Worldwide does not participate in, endorse, or have any authority or responsibility concerning private business transactions between our authors and the public.

All mail addressed to the author is forwarded but the publisher cannot, unless specifically instructed by the author, give out an address or phone number.

Any Internet references contained in this work are current at publication time, but the publisher cannot guarantee that a specific location will continue to be maintained. Please refer to the publisher's website for links to authors' websites and other sources.

Llewellyn Publications
A Division of Llewellyn Worldwide, Ltd.
2143 Wooddale Drive, Dept. 978-0-7387-1143-0
Woodbury, MN 55125-2989, U.S.A.
www.llewellyn.com

Printed in the United States of America

Other Books by Rowan Davis

The Ex Files
(Llewellyn Publications, 2007)

Upcoming Books by Rowan Davis

The Sex Files
(Llewellyn Publications, 2008)

Acknowledgments

For me, because I wanted to, and it was far better than boring myself to death. And thanks to my forgiving husband, without whom I never would have learned the correct way to squeeze the toothpaste tube.

Contents

Introduction / ix

The *Aries* Ex-Boyfriend . . . 3

The *Taurus* Ex-Boyfriend . . . 21

The *Gemini* Ex-Boyfriend . . . 39

The *Cancer* Ex-Boyfriend . . . 55

The *Leo* Ex-Boyfriend . . . 71

The *Virgo* Ex-Boyfriend . . . 87

The *Libra* Ex-Boyfriend . . . 103

The *Scorpio* Ex-Boyfriend . . . 121

The *Sagittarius* Ex-Boyfriend . . . 137

The *Capricorn* Ex-Boyfriend . . . 155

The *Aquarius* Ex-Boyfriend . . . 173

The *Pisces* Ex-Boyfriend . . . 189

Introduction

The dynamics of a breakup often are very complicated and hurtful. Deducing who's to blame, what can be done about it now, and whether there's a reason to feel guilty or betrayed can produce obsessive thoughts once a breakup has occurred. Understanding the astrology of the situation can give you a glimpse into these dynamics and help ease the pain and confusion surrounding the breakup. In the following pages, I give brief examples of what to expect from each sign after a breakup, how your own sign will handle it, and what you can do now.

As an ex, you must deal with the reality of playing a new role in your former lover's life. The bond the two of you shared and the right you had to know about his life and whereabouts are gone. Sometimes it's possible to create a friendship where romance once flourished, but sometimes too much resentment has built up or too much has happened between you for either to pretend that everything's okay. Either way, the changing of roles and the replacement of lovers is a difficult process. If you understand what hurdles you're facing and what to expect from your ex, then you're likely to escape with less pain and regret than you would have otherwise.

No matter what you decide to do now or how you choose to pull through, recovery is something we all can't help but do, for it's true that time heals all wounds. There always will be someone to love, and fate never shows us a glimpse of happiness without allowing us to make mistakes and then try again. If only we could be as forgiving of ourselves as life is with us! Then we could understand that pain teaches valuable lessons, mistakes are made, and those we once chose to idolize are beautiful for their humanity and not their divinity. It is human nature to despise and envy those who are "perfect"; we simply would rather not be near them. Oh, but the troubled, the hurting, and the ones who learn from their mistakes—in essence, the ones who promise us that we can succeed as they have succeeded—those are the ones we love. Similarly, every relationship begins with something good, such as desire, admiration, or adoration, and yet when it's over, we are so quick to condemn, demonize, personalize, and toss aside anything that was positive about it. The good has not disappeared, but we don't see it anymore because we no longer are looking for it.

We humans can talk ourselves into anything. Most of us use this ability to make ourselves believe that we are right and that our problems stem from other people and not ourselves. All signs are subject to this. Some are quick to recover from a breakup, and some are very slow. No matter what has happened or what sign you are, try to look at the world with the compassion you would give to yourself at your lowest moment and the joy you celebrate at your highest. Never forget that, on any given day, you can share, teach, and love people, or you can hate, resent, and ruin them. It's your choice. In the following pages, I present enough negativity associated with each sign that I hope your mind will rebel and start to remember all of the positive things that I have missed. Love is much more important than hate, although hate can be fun sometimes.

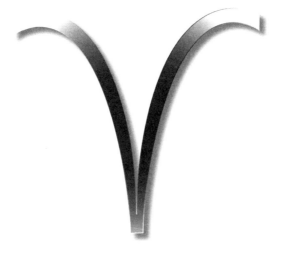

Aries

The *Aries* Ex-Boyfriend

Dates: March 21–April 20
Planet: Mars
Element: Cardinal fire
Representation: Ram

You might think that being the ex-girlfriend of an Aries will be easy; after all, he's been threatening to leave you since the two of you got together. Unfortunately, now that you are apart, he's not quite sure what to do with himself—especially if you were the one who initiated the breakup. Following the logic of the Aries male, he protected you from the embarrassment of all of your faults while the two of you were an item, and now that you are not, welcome to a no-holds-barred battle of wills, egos, and reputations. This is one man who doesn't enjoy failing at anything, and regardless of who is at fault for the ending of your affair, he will do his best to make sure the world sees that *you* are the one lacking in what it took to keep the relationship going.

As an infantile idealist, the Aries has been on the lookout for his Perfect Woman ever since he discovered that his mother had faults, and he probably attempted to mold you into this image of the ideal woman once or twice (can you say *understatement?*) during your relationship. Nothing you did was good enough for him, and he made sure you knew how generous and hopeful he was by staying with you anyway—despite all your flaws. Actually, when it really came down to it, he not only wanted your acknowledgment that he was a good person for remaining in a relationship with you, but he also demanded your devotion and even *reverence* because of it.

If there's one thing an Aries is good at, it's extracting a commitment from even the most hesitant of women. If you thought that dating an Aries male was difficult, you'll find that in the breakup he will attempt to engage you in such a way that if you were to blindly follow his lead, you'd end up even more involved and committed to him than you were when you two were an item, because now he's free to do what he wants while you remain his avid subject. This is a man who hates to have people dislike him, unless he can fathom a good reason for them doing so that leaves no doubt as to his superiority—such as if they are jealous. If you left him, then he has been made uncomfortably aware that there just might be something wrong with him or with something he did. He can't stand it. He is desperate for reassurance that on some level you still want him, and he will go to any length to prove to himself that you are the one with the problem.

As an ex, either he will pine over the loss of you and conveniently forget all the problems the two of you had, or he will add you as another notch on his belt and move on without a backward glance, except to gloat every once in a while about how much you wanted him and how heartbroken you are without him. Typically, you will get the former outcome if you were the one to leave and if it looks, to all observers, as though you are more than comfortable staying gone. You probably will get the latter outcome if you chase him, begging for the return of your lost Warrior. This doesn't mean that the Aries man is bereft of any true feeling; he just is unsure about how to show his emotions in a way that flatters him. He calls it being "stoic."

What You'll Miss

His childish innocence and charm. He was easy to hurt, and tried very hard to make sure that nobody knew it. He was a fiery lover, trying so hard to please you that your heart went out to him. He could be a brilliant conversationalist and probably was very intelligent. The way he desperately clung to his ego and his idealism made you feel protective. At first. If you're the type of woman who loves a virile man, then you'll definitely miss the Aries. However, if you prefer a more sensual lover, then you'll be better off looking elsewhere for a means to satisfy your needs.

What You Won't Miss

After the initial stage of the affair, his ego began to look pathetic. So did his impossible fantasies of the Perfect Woman (which probably have been personified by an ex, regardless of what she actually was like). Toward the end of your relationship, you got very tired of being told all of the ways that you needed to improve if you wanted him to stay. After hearing about it enough, you began to wonder: what exactly would be so bad about his leaving?

How to Get Him Back
(If, for Some Reason, You Want to Know)

Pretend (or don't pretend) that you're happy without him. If he sees other men trailing after you (as long as they are the right kind of men—i.e., ones that he can respect), then he will begin to notice your positive qualities again. If you really want him back, you will have to stay close enough to him so that he notices your happiness and attractiveness. However, don't keep up the charade for too long; once he makes it known that he wants the two of you to be lovers again, timidly reveal to him how lost you are without him.

If there's anything that can help you through the cardinal-fire test you're facing, it's a bottle of ibuprofen and a good set of earplugs. Remember, butting heads with a Ram can leave you with a nasty headache, if not a concussion. Another good thing to remember is: don't fret over the rumor mill that surrounds you. Whatever the Aries does, it will show you (and the world) more about him than about you. And with any luck, his constant barrage of complaints about you will inspire a few heroic crushes from his cute friends, and they will be more than willing to come to your rescue (*and* put him in his place).

How to Make Sure He Stays Gone

Either follow him around like a lost puppy or forget him entirely (preferably while moving on with someone better). If you decide to throw caution to the wind and beg him to come back to you, his ego will be gratified with absolutely no work or commitment on his part and he will lose interest. Conversely, if you move on, there is the possibility that you will reject him if he tries to rekindle the flame. Aries men prefer to be assured of their victories.

How Your Sign Will Handle the Situation

Aries

If there's anything that pisses off an Aries woman (and secretly breaks her heart), it's being told that she isn't good enough. Your relationship with the Aries male was passionate, and you understood each other very well; however, that didn't make it any easier dealing with both of your conflicting Ideal Mates. Yes, there were times when the two of you suspected that the other had an undeniable likeness to your Perfect One, and the few times that those Ideal Mates coincided were truly magical and memorable experiences. As for the Aries man's threats and assaults, he had better watch out because he's met his match in you. There's a chance that he's smart enough to have realized this already and will make sure to stay on your good side.

Taurus

Your calm nature helps you deal with the Aries temper. Yes, you were hurt by the breakup. Yes, you sometimes wonder what it would be like now if the two of you had never broken up. But that doesn't mean that you'll risk your heart again by going back to him. After all, you tried your hardest to keep things going while the two of you were together, so what is there left to do now that you're apart? His foolish protection of his ego, and any damage he tries to inflict on yours, will be easy for you to deal with. After all, you are too pragmatic to be caught in his traps. Go out, flirt a little with no strings attached, and have fun. Commitment can wait for one more day, and Mr. Right is still out there somewhere other than in the rearview mirror. This time, try looking for someone more stable.

Gemini

There's a good chance that you already are moving on. The fiery Aries was an interesting companion, but now your rational mind has had time to grasp the fact that without him you are a much freer person. More than most other signs, the Aries is a *constant* companion, and one that jealously guards all of his possessions. While being one of his possessions seemed kind of kinky and comfortable at first, by the end of the affair it started to get downright claustrophobic. As for his attempts at defamation, you have a bigger mouth than he does and a stronger windpipe. You're a rare Gemini if you doubt that you'll ever find someone better, and you're even more unique if you refuse to look. Someone less clingy and a little more emotionally self-aware ought to be a welcome relief.

Cancer

Things weren't easy for the two of you. In the beginning, you seemed like the perfect pair—he was so manly and protective, and you were so softly feminine and nurturing. After a while, he found out that your feminine physique hid a steely cardinal sign, and there aren't many cardinals who are willing to follow someone else's lead for long. The Aries game of provoking jealousy in order to create a passionate response left you exhausted and hurt. To make matters worse, the Aries male was confused by your hurt reaction and responded with belittling comments about your lack of devotion rather than the reassuring words you needed. Now that the two of you are separated, your need for security probably has intensified. You'd do better backing off than begging for his return. Look for security within yourself.

Leo

A dangerous parting. The two of you had a serious chemical connection that now could easily turn into an explosive situation. Both of you will try to outdo each other when it comes to who can divulge the other's most shameful secrets the quickest, and fits of rage and jealousy will abound on both sides. If neither of you realizes the unhealthy game you're playing, then both of you risk losing friendships as your friends grow weary of being involved in the bickering. Be the first to humble yourself and apologize for the meanness, and you'll come out the victor in the end, because the Aries won't know what to do with you. Decide if it's the game you love or the end result, and either find another player or look for Mr. Submissive. I have no doubt that once you find him (or them), you'll have little trouble adding him to your pride.

Virgo

He wanted you to be devoted no matter what and applaud his gallantry even when he was at his basest. You just couldn't do that. Mindless devotion and baseless applause are not in your natural-born repertoire of personality traits, although he doesn't understand that. He resented you because you wouldn't follow him like a puppy and wag your tail every time he opened the door to let you out. On a positive note, you will have an easier time dealing with the Aries as an ex than would many other women. You're sure of all of the reasons the two of you broke up, and you have a list a mile long of all his faults. Unless he has a strong Virgin influence somewhere else in his chart, there's little chance that his list for you (yes, he keeps his own records on people's faults, just in case) is as carefully thought out and recorded as is yours, which means you have a lot more ammunition than he does. Not that you'll get stuck in a war with an Aries. Still, you're bound to have a little skirmish now and again and when you do, such a list of his faults will come in handy. You're more than capable of winning these verbal duels.

Libra

Even with your incredible powers of tact and charm, you won't be able to avoid the Aries onslaught for long. Eventually he'll discover that your guise of continued devotion and admiration is false, and his anger will be even harsher because you duped him; he doesn't understand or care that you were only trying to keep from hurting him. If he's the one who left you, then he'll be appalled at how quickly you appear to recover (even if it takes you months or years to fully recover—he doesn't think that any woman should be able to get over him, ever). On some level, the two of you share some heavy karmic burdens, not to mention a continued attraction—despite the issues you have. Neither of you can help it: his Aries plays too well to your Aphrodite. Even though you can't help it, try to remember what drove you apart, because it'll still be there if you get back together.

Scorpio

On a psychological level, the two of you had some major problems to work out. You tend to be secretive, and the Aries hates to think that there's anything in the world he doesn't know about (even if he can admit on an intellectual level that there must be). Having a lover who keeps secrets brings the harsh truth a little too close to home, and he doesn't like it. Also, both you and the Aries can be spiteful if hurt. He knows how jealous you can get and isn't afraid to use it against you. I know that you feel betrayed and angry, but letting *him* know may be your undoing—or your best bet for a secure breakup. Be as honest as you can about your separation and he'll have difficulty pinning it on you. Find yourself a more stable partner, encourage him to do the same, and continue as friends if you can. Yes, the sting of a Scorpion can be deadly, but wouldn't you rather save your venom for a more worthy opponent?

Sagittarius

It's hard to imagine what would break up such a compatible duo. Maybe it was his ego or his inability to get a jealous rise out of you. Perhaps it was because of your independence and his need to be worshiped. Despite whatever led the two of you to this point, the breakup shouldn't be too bad. I said shouldn't be, not won't be—the two of you tend to be too unpredictable for anything to be guaranteed. There's a good chance of remaining friends because you have such an unusual tolerance for rumors and badmouthing; once he hits a nerve, you'll let him know in a way that he's able to take without being offended. If he left you, then he'll be kinder about it than if you were another sign. You're not likely to go running after him. Chasing a Ram really isn't your style, and it would only embarrass you both.

Capricorn

When a female Capricorn sets her mind to do something or to believe in something, she sets it with the permanence of a mountain. It's hard to move on to another relationship once you've gone to the trouble of convincing yourself that this one is worth fighting for, that this is the one you need. Of course, if you never got that far, then you won't have a hard time of moving on at all—you've been expecting that you would need to. Hopefully your change of mind about Mr. Aries was a gradual awakening to his faults rather than an abrupt decision on his part. Either way, both of you fought with all the strength of will that two cardinal signs can muster. He was as all-consuming as his fire element can make him, and you were steadfast and sturdy. Compromises weren't easy, and there still are quite a few resentments floating around. Now that the end has come and gone, you're not too concerned about what he's doing. You'll cringe at every rumor you hear, and your heart will break a few more times, but eventually you'll recover. And when you do, the world will be waiting for your next move.

Aquarius

If this jerk thinks he can verbally puke all over your reputation, then he's got another thing coming. You aren't one to sit by idly while someone tries to ruin the image that you've tried so hard to maintain. However, because you have worked as hard as you have, if you allow yourself to sit back and let him burn himself out, your cultivated reputation easily will withstand the assault. Hell, it might even help further your status, because the more men you have talking about you, the more people will hear about you, and the more your reputation will grow and lies eventually will be corrected or forgotten. Try to remember the ease with which the two of you communicated once upon a time, and calmly let him know when he's hurt you, and even more calmly ask him not to do it again. Aries always tries to be the hero—a maiden's plea is not cast aside lightly, especially if he loved her.

Pisces

Hmm. This all depends on what your relationship was like. If he took care of you, took responsibility for you, then the breakup will be mild. He'll be unhappy and without purpose, but you're more resilient than you let on. The Aries plays a perfect hero to your maiden in distress, perpetrator to your victim, and even if he was overprotective of you during your relationship, he can't help but deliver a couple of low blows now. If your relationship was tempestuous, full of accusations and misunderstandings, then it won't be much different now, despite the mutual relief about the parting. You'll end up spending a lot of time at the bottom of your personal ocean, waiting for the histrionics to pass. There's a good chance that you already have your eye on someone new—go, have fun, and wave at the Aries as you pass him by.

Taurus

The *Taurus* Ex-Boyfriend

Dates: April 21–May 21
Planet: Venus / Pan-Horus
Element: Fixed earth
Representation: Bull

It's quite an amusing sight when a Bull gets his horns stuck in his own rear end—especially when it was *your* posterior he was aiming at. True, most Bulls would rather romp alone in their pasture, musing over their shortcomings, than cause any type of confrontation with an ex. (You see, their pride is already hurt, and they don't want to risk any further damage.) But when one of them decides to charge the fence and run through the local village, or through the cow pasture, real damage can be done. They are possessive, simple men who make a point to care only about a few things in life, like family, food, and fu…making love.

The Taurus man usually is traditionally minded. If you want to be his spouse for long, you must have the ability to cook a good meal, look pretty while you're cleaning the toilet, keep silent when his sports are on TV, and be content with being little more than his status symbol/housemaid. If this is the kind of life you're looking for, then go find yourself an earth sign ASAP; however, if you burned your bra long ago, and have since made amends with it but not with the misogynistic patriarchy you sought to overthrow once upon a time, it'll be good for your psyche to leave this man far behind. He is possessive, jealous, and a homebody, which means you'll never leave the house unless it's for some same-sex, traditionally accepted activity like shopping.

If you've ever doubted that fixed earth is constrictive, then you've never squeezed between two heavy boulders and thought about the issue. Fixed earth is hard, cold, previously volcanic granite. Mountains with granite cores get worn down *around the granite*. Both of the other earth signs, Capricorn and Virgo, will erode into sand long before Taurus even cracks. So to be surrounded by fixed earth is to be encased in one of the hardest naturally made materials on the planet. Yes, air and water eventually will begin to wear away a Taurus, but it will take a while. If you've been through a long relationship with a Bull, then none of this should come as a surprise to you. You know how restrictive he could be. You understand the contradictions and dangers of this man's personality—on the one hand so stable and domesticated, and on the other so violently aggressive and stubborn. Now that you've ended your relationship with the Taurus, you'll be able to look back at what once was, stretch your arms wide, go out for a run (without the fear of a Bull charging you), and bask in your newfound freedom.

As an ex, the Taurus usually is too busy nursing his wounded pride and broken heart to worry about what you're doing, and there is a large part of him that really doesn't want to know what you're up to. He'll be hurt when you move on, but here is a man who's capable of being happy if you're happy. He'll be honest about what happened in your relationship, but he won't go out of his way to spread rumors or ruin your reputation. Of course, all this is null and void if you push him into doing something. Ever tried pushing a Bull? It's slowgoing, especially if you're doing all you can to aggravate him, to hurt his pride and show him that he was never good enough for you. Once he's been pushed too far, watch out for that legendary Taurus temper.

To survive having the Bull as an ex, you will need to make sure you don't wear anything red on a windy day when you're going to be around him. Deep inside, the Bull is insecure and afraid that, if he showers you with affection or shows you how upset he is at your leaving, you will take his heart and mutilate it beyond recognition. Perhaps that seems like fitting revenge for all the crap he put you through and for how unbelievably self-centered and tradition-bound he was. It's your choice. But it's always better to move on to something new than to be stuck in the past.

What You'll Miss

The Bull is one of the most reliable signs in the zodiac. He is stability incarnate. Though he lacked somewhat in the romance department, he more than made up for it in bed (and at the dining table). He was proud of you and let everyone know it. He also provided a comfortable environment and was willing to support you financially.

What You Won't Miss

All that crap about you being "his little woman." He just ignored anything he didn't want to deal with, and he always made excuses for everyone (and mostly himself) unless either they questioned his authority or he needed to climb over them on his way up the corporate or social ladder. The leash he gave you was short enough for you to choke on every once in a while, and although security has its value, so does a true partnership based on devotion and freedom.

How to Get Him Back
(If, for Some Reason, You Want to Know)

What the Taurus prizes above everything else is security; however, his heart comes in a close second. When your relationship appeared to have ended, he took it as proof that his heart wasn't safe with you. The Taurus either wants eternal love or momentary sexual relief. If you want to reclaim his heart, you must convince him that you will never break it again. Don't push too hard, but make your availability and desire known.

How to Make Sure He Stays Gone

I know it isn't a natural thing to do to a wounded Bull, but you need to turn your back on him and walk away. Make a declaration about what your needs are and all the ways that he doesn't satisfy them and then leave, no matter what he says to try to get you to stay. Because the Bull hates begging or looking weak, it isn't very hard to see that he'll leave you alone—once you're already gone. It's really the going part that's difficult.

How Your Sign Will Handle the Situation

Aries

Not one who is used to a short leash, you'll be glad to have your freedom back. Of course, there's that little pang in your chest every time you think about him and the solidity he provided, which you secretly crave. At least your tempestuous relationship was interesting, and the Taurus man was adept at protecting you from yourself and your inner demons. If you're looking for a way to stop missing him, go out and enjoy your freedom a little. You and the Taurus share a bond through Aries and Aphrodite that ensures a continued, ill-fated attraction, despite the obstacles the two of you encounter. A breakup will be either a final, karmic conclusion or just another problem, neither the first nor the last.

Taurus

It's curious to think about what would lead a dependable Taurus to leave another dependable Taurus. Maybe…hmm…boredom? Or maybe it was something far more reasonable, like your mutual possessiveness got in the way, or the traditions he catered to were not your own. Perhaps the sex got stale. For whatever reason, the two of you are no longer an item, and it shouldn't worry you too much. Yes, it rocked your foundation a little, and a Taurus heart takes some time to heal. Neither of you really sees the benefit in ridiculing the other, even if some resentments exist. It's much easier, and far more reasonable, to do the conventional thing—move on to someone else, pay more attention to your career, etc. Why waste energy hating and screaming and waging a war in which the winner is more a perception than an actuality?

Gemini

It's hard to predict how you will handle the breakup when no one's exactly sure how the two of you ended up together in the first place. All in all, you probably will handle the breakup better than you handled being confined and possessed by the Taurus male, unless...The Taurus has a tendency to become valuable because of what he represents, and if the two of you break up, you will lose not only him but also what he represents to you. That could be a good thing or a bad thing. As a Gemini, you rarely have trouble walking away from anyone, but...No matter how you look at it, being the Gemini you are, it will be easy to find one or two or ten other guys to take the Bull's place. Maybe someone who wants to come along for the ride would be better next time?

Cancer

A Taurus and a Cancer can be a strangely soothing pair. Both of you were homebodies, enjoyed security, and wanted stability. But there were a few little things that drove each of you nuts: he was so gruff and standoffish sometimes, and your emotional shifts unsettled him. He didn't spend much energy trying to understand your moods, and in fact there wasn't much that he tried to understand. Oh, he dealt with things, but *dealing* is a lot different than *comprehending*; as a Cancer, you intuit the difference. And when people don't understand you, you tend to take it personally and retreat into your protective shell. This didn't help things with the Taurus, because a Taurus thinks that if he doesn't hear about a problem, then there is no problem. Now that the two of you have parted, the ending won't be terribly harsh or hurtful. You'll both be upset, but when a Taurus and a Cancer part, there's a feeling of lost opportunity in the air.

Leo

How exactly does a vibrant, passionate Lioness become involved with a stiff, conservative Bull? What exactly made you settle for someone lower on the food chain? Hope, the love of a challenge, the Bull's devotion, and your own loyalty are just a few possible reasons. After a while, though, it felt as though your independent Lioness was being turned into a mere house cat. Now that you're free from restriction, nature can return to its normal state: lions eat cattle, and cattle run. Just remember, the Bull is no ordinary bovine. As an ex, he's unlikely to run around irrationally attacking your reputation, although he might huff and puff when you start seeing someone new. Don't take his outward acceptance of the breakup as a sign that what you two shared wasn't important to him—it was. The thing is, he's already spotted the lush pasture next door. Remember to close the gate behind him.

Virgo

You're lucky that your talent for organizing and list making has led you to become overly familiar with the Bull's shortcomings; otherwise, the natural affinity the two of you have for one another would make it difficult for you to be without him. You are a strong woman, and having the Taurus man around seemed to add to your strength rather than detract from it. Despite the mutual attraction, the two of you may not have had the easiest time. Your own practicality clashed with his stubborn support of outdated thoughts and actions. His acceptance of your willingness to cook, clean, and generally take care of him eventually turned into him taking you for granted. A friendship can be retained now that your relationship is over; however, the Taurus eventually will look for physical passion from you if you stick around.

Libra

The power struggle between you and the Taurus could be severe at times, even if it was hidden under the guise of his nonchalance and your tactfulness. You are a cardinal sign and he is a Bull, so neither of you gives up your goals or beliefs easily. While both of you technically share Venus as a ruler, there isn't much of a likeness between you. You are a social butterfly and a cardinal sign, and you don't like being caged—even if the bars are made of gold. The Taurus prefers to stay close to home and doesn't want to deal with the intricacies of human behavior in social situations. Now that the two of you are apart, your diplomacy and his stoicism will help keep you from engaging in open warfare. You will remember the good times, but unless you have compatible Ascendants or Moon signs, your goodbyes will be permanent.

Scorpio

You and the Taurus are astrological opposites, which accounts for much of the strange attraction you had for each other. Now that you're apart, there's a certain lack of closure and a curiosity about what could have been. At first, both of you will be happy to be rid of the other. Being astrological opposites permeates your interactions with the unyielding Bull with an air of desperation, anxiety, and loss, making you both uncomfortable. Neither of you will be happy when the other finds someone new, and both of you eventually will move on. While you might have an urge to defame the stolid Taurus male, it will be better if you just move on without fighting, especially because he's unlikely to do anything openly against you first. Your Scorpion passions run near the surface, so opposite the Taurean block of granite that once sat on your living room sofa.

Sagittarius

Well, you knew that you were a wanderer and that the Taurus was a little too attached to his couch. He never was happy that you wouldn't let him know about your adventures; he felt like you were keeping something from him in order to maintain control of your relationship. The Taurus demands ownership of his lovers, but he never could find a price tag on you, and he doubted that you'd give your love away for free. Now that you're apart (and his worst fears have been validated), your diplomacy and charm allow you to understand your differences without getting upset about them, and to calm his hurt feelings a little. You understand that he will find someone new, the sooner the better, and he's always known on some level that he couldn't hold on to you forever. His stability gave you a wonderful jumping-off point, but what happens after the leap?

Capricorn

Both of you understand the value of money and status, and it's difficult to let each other go. But the similarities were a little too endless, and there was some chance of boredom. Now that you're without him, you're free to walk to your own beat once again. Neither of you is into spreading rumors or demonizing your exes, and you are more than capable of remaining friends after the breakup—as long as you each deal with any lingering resentments and watch out for each other's feelings. A breakup is never really pain-free, but yours has a good chance of being easier than most. Still, both of you are possessive people, and neither will be too happy when the other moves on, even if you pretend to be. Whatever little quirks or misunderstandings initially drove you apart, the decision to end the relationship permanently—and how—will be well thought out and carefully planned on both sides.

Aquarius

Both of you are highly practical people with a streak of sentimentality and a stubborn idea of just how things should be, as well as a dislike for giving up control. Fixed air and fixed earth make for a wonderful science experiment, but not such a great relationship. In many ways, air is a more dangerous element than earth: air can change earth by constantly pelting it with its own crap, yet earth can only change the direction of air and create a space that it cannot get to. You, more than any other sign in the zodiac, will be able to cow the raging Bull. However, as a person who doesn't enjoy being cowed, he might surprise you with his vengeance. Playing with a sleeping Bull isn't something that anyone should venture into lightly. Now that he's your ex, it would be best if both of you just drop the weapons and back away slowly. He's a threat only if you let him be.

Pisces

Because the Taurus was a functional anchor in your life, you're feeling a little out of control now that he's gone (even if you were feeling a little too controlled while you were together). Although you enjoy your newfound sexual freedom, you long for the money and constancy he provided. What you won't miss is the restrictive hold he had on your fantasies. For some reason, he always tried to bring you back to reality, and being grounded constantly without any protective water to swim in can leave a Fish gasping for breath. Of course, he didn't understand that. The Bull has difficulty trying to understand anything he doesn't agree with—yet another reason the two of you didn't work out. While it's easy to be submissive, next time you'd be better off finding someone more on your wavelength and more willing to see your point of view.

Gemini

The *Gemini* Ex-Boyfriend

Dates: May 22–June 21
Planet: Mercury
Element: Mutable air
Representation: Twins

When it comes to the Twins' true feelings about you and the breakup, his explanations can get rather long-winded. He isn't too sure himself about how he feels. What he does know is that the situation is tragic, and he's unsure of exactly how he'll ever manage to live without you. Surprising? For a man who spent most of his time either in a fantasy world or trying to assert his independence in other ways, he certainly is heartbroken now. But is he really? If your relationship was a committed one, one that he seemed to enjoy and be as interested in as you were, then his depression and moping around are probably authentic, and he's honestly busy ruminating on all his shortcomings. I hate to say it, but it's not exactly *you* that he's missing—he's just getting caught up in the drama and playing the role as passionately as he can. It's the tragedy that calls him, as tragedy means he's lost you. And if he's lost you, then he doesn't have to try to keep you anymore, and it was the keeping of you that concerned him. Now he's free to be passionately in love with you without any of the responsibilities. Lovely, isn't it? However, if the relationship never was very serious, then he'll leave you with all of the delicacy of an elephant tap dancing. And he won't look back.

In either case, he no longer has a need to protect your feelings. Sure, his depression might lead him to hope that you'll come back, but hurting you will increase his own pain and make the heartbreak even more vibrant. He'll start bragging to you about his conquests as if you were a regular friend of his who has no residual emotional interests or concerns. You knew he did this with others, because it drove you crazy that he was still friends with his exes and that he treated them like they were one of the guys—and sometimes it's hard to sit placidly across from someone who knows what your man looks like naked and tied up with ropes (especially because you can tell by his eyes that he remembers it too). Despite the fact that he isn't worried about hurting you anymore, and even though Gemini is the communicator of the zodiac, he'll be careful about whom he chooses to divulge your secrets to. He doesn't want to get in a fight with you; he just wants to feel the pain of your loss. Ruining your reputation won't do anything for him when he either has left you far behind or is humbly awaiting your return.

At times, it seems as though a Gemini male exists for no other purpose than to sell things and ideas to people who don't necessarily need them. In fact, he's so busy trying to convince people of his "ideas" that he often loses sight of the core truth. Plus, he changes his own mind in seconds flat. This is where he gets his classic mercurial reputation. It's also how he convinces himself that a woman he once thought held him prisoner now seems like the only key to his salvation. As flattering as this may sound to you, remind yourself of how easy it is for the Gemini mind to morph you instantly from a Venus into a hag. I hate to burst your bubble like this, but it might save you from many months of misery and confusion trying to figure out what it is that he *really* wants from you and your relationship. That's not to say that there aren't *any* Gemini men out there who can honestly learn the error of their ways and make permanent changes for the better.

Despite the intensity of his emotions immediately after the breakup, he eventually will move on, and it will be like you never existed. There comes a point in every Gemini's life when he simply forgets anything he'd rather not remember. In fact, he reaches this point on an almost daily basis.

What You'll Miss

The Gemini male was highly entertaining. He was always up to something. He was a talkative partner who was glad to discuss anything—as long as it was something he was interested in, which was just about everything, aside from boring, routine topics like work and finances. He was charming and loved to compliment you. His little-boy charisma was irresistible, and his unconventionality added excitement to the bedroom.

What You Won't Miss

His complete lack of ambition and drive meant that you had to either support him or follow him down the rabbit hole. Even if he wasn't technically unfaithful, he often let you know that he was interested in other women, and his constant flirting eventually gave you a nervous twitch. His fickleness had you running in circles, and you never knew what to believe.

How to Get Him Back
(If, for Some Reason, You Want to Know)

Flattery, kindness, and continued friendship eventually will lead him your way again. Always keep yourself just out of reach, but tease him a lot. Boost his ego and he'll be yours forever. Flaunt your desirability, intrigue him, and talk to him a lot about subjects he enjoys. It isn't hard to attract this man, but it's hard to keep him in one place once you've got him. Become his playful partner in crime and don't overly restrict him, and he'll be as happy as he can be.

How to Make Sure He Stays Gone

It's not hard to make a Gemini go away—most of the time he does it all on his own. If for some reason he won't leave of his own accord, then let him know, in no uncertain terms, that the two of you will never be together again. At first, this will make him chase after you even more, but once he gets the idea, he'll leave you alone. The easiest way to get rid of him is to stop caring about him. He's so charming and childish that you've probably gotten used to having to take care of him. Stop it. Now. And don't care about what happens to him afterward.

How Your Sign Will Handle the Situation

Aries

While his changeable mind and new ideas kept you on your toes mentally, physical and emotional passion from him were wanting (when judged by the standards of a fire sign). His lack of possessiveness left you with the impression that he just didn't care, and his wanderlust elicited your own ever-ready jealousy. Tempers ran high, but now that he's gone, you're wondering if you tried hard enough. You did. Don't worry, it's just that closure is hard to find when it comes to the Twins. Also, the two of you were too different in some very important areas: possessiveness, loyalty, passion, and love, to name just a few. After the breakup, the Gemini is apt to talk badly about you only to certain people, and you aren't likely to ever hear about it unless his friends are egging him on.

Taurus

What probably hurts the most is wondering why he wasn't content with you. You cooked for him and cleaned his apartment, and yet he still would snap at you every once in a while and leave for days on end. You didn't do anything wrong, and he could have been very happy with you—as much as any Gemini allows himself to be happy. When your Gemini ex says, "It's not you, it's me," believe him, because the breakup has a lot more to do with him than with you. Now that he's gone (and probably off on another of his stupid adventures), you finally are free to find someone who is closer to your Ideal Companion. If Mr. Gemini truly cared for you, then he'll be happy when you find that person. There's little chance for much end-of-romance drama between you. You're too mature for it, and he's too gone.

Gemini

Maybe the two of you had opposing tastes in wine and that seemed as good a thing to fight about as any. With this ex-pairing, it's difficult to say what happened—or will happen. The trouble isn't just the sheer number of you involved—you, him, your Twin, his Twin—it's also in the fact that it takes a Gemini to fully understand another Gemini, causing the two of you to have more emotions wrapped up in one another than most rock bands. Either you will easily be able to remain friends, because neither of you is the jealous type and both of you ended things on a good note, or you will be wildly upset with one another and hurt when the other moves on, and will wallow miserably in your individual tragedies. Or perhaps you'll just get bored and need a change. No matter what happens in the end, or the middle, or even the beginning, you'll be fine. The road may be a little rocky, but you'll manage. You always do.

Cancer

Even though there was something fascinating about the Gemini male, and you loved all the compliments he paid you, you couldn't get over the lack of security in this relationship. His flirtatiousness hurt you on many occasions. He never was very good at making you feel better, and his charm made you feel manipulated. While you understood him on an innate level, your relationship was ripe with misunderstandings and resentments. However, each of you had an important lesson to teach the other: you could learn to be a little more relaxed, and he could stand to be a little less so. As an ex, he'll make a good friend; however, boundaries need to be set concerning just how much info he should give you about his new fling and whether you will ever meet her. There will always be an attraction between you and Mr. Gemini; so be aware that long after the two of you have split, he or his double may show up at your door needing a place to stay because his "new" ex has kicked him out. Can you say "sofa bed"?

Leo

There's a lot of unfinished business between the two of you. You had hoped that this daring socialite would enhance your image, but his true nature revealed itself and on some level you were sorely disappointed. He never lived up to what you thought he was before you got involved with each other, and now that you're apart you won't think twice about letting everyone else know it. He's so timid when faced with your brilliance that, unless he has some powerful backup, he'll turn into a ball of pitiable fluff whenever you're around. It won't be long until you've found someone to more than replace this King of Masks, and you won't be getting the worst of the bargain, either. There is some major astrological karmic stuff going on between the two of you, so pay attention to important interactions or cycles and be aware that this might not be the last you see of him. There's something for you to learn here.

Virgo

There always was some strain in your relationship. The Gemini is so unconventional, and you are so…well…*conventional*. That doesn't mean there never was any positive spark; however, you share Mercury as a ruling planet (for now, at least, until your own Vulcan planet is discovered), which gives you a certain attraction to, and understanding of, one another. But *understanding* doesn't mean *accepting*. Virgos, unfortunately, always seem to go for the least stable guy in the room. Bet you think you'll be able to change his roaming ways. True, you have a better chance of changing a Gemini than most girls do. But there's something about him that resists any change, despite his apparent longing for it. Now that you two are finished, you'll be able to maintain a friendship, because both of you can accept your differences as long as you don't have to live with them.

Libra

Well, it's a little late to say that you make a good pair, but in a strange, intellectual way, you did. In fact, astrologically speaking, the two of you were perfect for each other. Both of you are intelligent, rational thinkers who love attention and freedom and yet secretly long for a fateful commitment. One downside was that he had a lot more to learn from you than you from him, and you like to partner with men who will enhance you in some way rather than detract. The fact that you are one of the few women to get under his skin makes it difficult for him to let you go and easy for you to use your charm to stay on good terms with him. As an ex, he'll be jealous and upset if you find someone else (and Librans *always* find someone else), but he'll be more willing to maintain a friendship with you than he would be with other signs.

Scorpio

While the two of you were together, the Gemini's fickleness and wandering eye made you question his fidelity. And if there's anything a Scorpio hates (and yet is prone to), it's fearing that her man is unfaithful. Unfortunately, there is reason to fear when it comes to a Gemini, as you may have found out. Even the most faithful Mercurial man is apt to flirt with anyone who crosses his path, and while he might not have any intention of cheating, the person he's flirting with doesn't know that. As an ex, you'll still be bothered by his romantic escapades (if you still allow yourself to be aware of them), and there's a vindictive part of the Gemini that knows this and savors it. While you might miss him, at least you're free now to find someone more loyal and trustworthy, which will put your mind at ease.

Sagittarius

Oh, how many adventures the two of you had! Both of you are charismatic travelers with lots of stories to tell. However, that didn't make things easy between you. When it comes to love, you are so optimistic that you easily can be led astray by a Gemini male—and he isn't exactly forthcoming about his intentions. A breakup between the two of you won't be as difficult as with many other pairs. Neither of you is an extreme gossip; the Gemini will carefully pick out the people to whom he'll talk negatively about you, and you'll be quiet (maybe a few quick jabs here and there) while you plot his demise. And just because he's talking and you're plotting doesn't mean that either of you will inflict much damage. Both of you have your own lives to get back to.

Capricorn

The good news is that you have one horn for each of the Gemini Twins, and if you rush at him head-on, you're sure to hit both of them…maybe. He was everything that made you feel insecure and annoyed, and as you aren't one of the signs that easily falls for his manipulations, it's hard to imagine how the two of you got together in the first place. Maybe it was his social connections or his energy. No matter what attracted you to him to begin with, and what problems you had during your relationship, you're probably at least a little hurt now that you've broken up—though you'll never let him know. And if he tries anything, in a battle of wills, your rock-hard strength of character will easily outlast his Mercury vapors. You'll have an easy time of moving on to someone better and more stable. You just need to give love another chance.

Aquarius

Because of the shared air element, the two of you have a very good chance of handling this breakup well. You and the Gemini understand each other on a deep level. You both know what each of you wants in life, and you are rather selfless in hoping that he gets it. You also are one of the few people who can predict what he'll do, and the anticipation of an event can reduce its impact. For example, you know he'll find another lover soon, so when he does, it won't come as a surprise. However, if he didn't learn to stay on your good side while the two of you were together, then he'll definitely get the lesson now. You don't like being made to look like a fool, and Geminis typically respond to being hurt by making jokes. Luckily, there is a strong possibility that the two of you will be able to maintain a friendship. You won't appreciate his bragging, but you'll have plenty of your own to do—if you want to.

Pisces

From the start, you had a feeling this was going to end, and you have a knack for sensing these things. (If only you'd learn to trust your instincts!) The two of you were too different, although at times you fascinated each other. Eventually, what brought you together tore you apart: his intellect and your fantasies, his carefree attitude and your feminine charms. Now that you're separated, there are plenty of negative feelings on both sides. While your tact and willingness to continue a friendship will help keep things from becoming too hurtful, the Gemini eventually will feel used and manipulated and will strike out against you. A definitive breakup would be better for both of you in the long run. Chances are, you already had someone else in line when this relationship fell through, and if not, someone will come along shortly.

Cancer

The *Cancer* Ex-Boyfriend

Dates: June 22–July 22
Planet: Moon
Element: Cardinal water
Representation: Crab

When you were a couple, you noticed that the Cancer had some very strong attachments. First off, he is very devoted to his friends. All of his friends. Even the troubled, beautiful young women who turn to him for romantic advice…and attention. Although his own jealousy is legendary, he was confused when you got upset after he spent all night at a woman's house, holding her while she cried, ignoring your phone calls, and doing who knows what else to make her feel better. After all, it's his job to help people, and he won't stop being a *good friend* just because his own lover doesn't understand. In fact, if you insisted on misunderstanding the situation, then he probably felt like he needed to turn to his friends for a little advice and attention of his own. Could you blame him? Hell yes, you can. If you're bent on vengeance, his "chivalry" leaves a perfect opening for some spite, and he's never too naïve or humble to see it coming.

Another of his attachments is to his dear, sweet mother. Wherever the Crab is, his mother is close by. It's pretty common to find her either timidly walking somewhere behind him or demandingly leading him. Regardless of her exact location, she'll be there…somewhere. Whether you guessed it while the two of you were together or the realization came after your breakup, you see now how a lot of his insecurities came from his mother, and you know that he won't be able to grow as a person until the umbilical cord has been cut. In fact, learning how to grow, evolve, and become independent are particularly important tasks for the Cancer incarnation.

If you expect some of the sweetness he showed you while the two of you were together to somehow carry over into your breakup, then you're right—it will. What you might not expect (and what you might not have noticed while you were with him) is that his sweetness is a manipulative ploy to extract your obedience and continued loyalty while protecting him from any unpleasant confrontations. The all-consuming shell of the Crab closes his mind to the possibility that other ways of thinking and feeling are out there, and he simply doesn't understand your unexpected emotions, so he ignores them. Whether the hand that reaches out to him intends to take him out of harm's way or put him in a boiling pot, his instinctual reaction is the same—a quick withdrawal into his protective shell. The problem is that he can't trust anything outside of himself, and his own feelings and thoughts are the only ones he's comfortable with. If anyone brings up anything that conflicts with his internal dialogue, he'll retreat, ponder the issue, and usually toss aside the other person's viewpoint because he's the only one who really understands the situation.

It's a tight fit being squeezed into the shell of a Crab. Those shells usually are made to fit only one animal, and yet he expected you to somehow be comfortable. Well, even if it wasn't roomy, at least it was secure (a straightjacket isn't roomy either, but it usually keeps the occupant in line). Sweet, sensitive, and utterly impenetrable, the Cancerian ex-boyfriend has a nasty tendency to slowly eat away at you without you even knowing he's doing it. You've probably heard that the male Cancer can be quite sentimental and that this adds to his reputation of being a sensitive and caring lover. Well, it also adds to his predisposition to be cruel to his exes. He holds on to them, tugging ruthlessly at their hearts whenever he senses that they are about to get away, just in case the breakup was a mistake that he'll need to correct in the future. Sometimes, even years later, a Cancerian ex will turn up on your doorstep with two dozen roses and a sappy grin, stoically ignoring your fiancé and wedding planner.

What You'll Miss

Boyish and fun-loving, he also was protective and highly imaginative. He knew how to make you feel comfortable and secure. He seemed to understand the need you had for a classic romance, and he always made you feel like you were the belle of the ball and the only woman in his heart—besides his mother.

What You Won't Miss

His clinginess reminded you of walking across a carpeted room, petting a cat while wearing a silk skirt. No matter how hard you tried to loosen the skirt's grip, it just kept riding up your butt. His romance and loyalty didn't exactly keep him monogamous, as the Cancer has an annoying tendency to sample the other possibilities while he's considering leaving you (not that he'll ever own up to any of it). His defensiveness made him very difficult to talk to, and his jealousy and insecurity made it hard to go anywhere.

How to Get Him Back
(If, for Some Reason, You Want to Know)

It's harder than you'd imagine it to be, seeing as how he clings to his exes. He is a terribly insecure man and is very sensitive to imagined (or unimagined) slights. He already knows that a rekindled relationship with you has a pretty good chance of failing, and the thought of risking his heart again makes him uncomfortable. However, his sentimentality will grow with time, and usually he will be the one who makes the effort to return and repair what once was. It will be up to you to decide if taking the chance is worth it.

How to Make Sure He Stays Gone

Hurt his ego whenever you can. He will resent having to retreat into his protective shell every time you're around, and eventually he'll start avoiding you. That way he's unlikely to feel very sentimental about you and what could have been. However, you'll also come across as a total bitch to anyone you're around. It's not your fault; it's just hard to get the point across to a guy who is as self-centered as the Cancer is. He simply doesn't take hints well, unless the hint matches his own suspicions and assumptions, and right now he's too busy trying to turn his memories of you into a timeless love tragedy.

How Your Sign Will Handle the Situation

Aries

Mr. Cancer was an enigma. He wanted you all to himself, and yet when it came time to fight for you, he did little more than retreat into his shell and stew about it. His pathetic, cowardly withdrawal made you sick to your stomach. You want your men to be stronger than you and to be able to stand up to anything you or the world throws at them, not to cower at home, waiting for the trouble to pass. You thrive on conquests and winning, and he tries his hardest to keep out of everyone's way and not to upset anyone. The fact that the Cancer's ego is a defense rather than a personality trait conflicted with your own all-too-ready pride and led to some major resentments and arguments. And now he wants to put you on a shelf just in case you come in handy in the future? I don't think so, and it would be better for him if he didn't think so either.

Taurus

This is one of those breakups that leaves everyone feeling a little lost and betrayed. Both of you need security and stability in a relationship, and the fact that trust has been broken and that hopes have been dissolved doesn't make either of you feel good about the situation. Whereas the Crab might want to come back later for seconds, you tend to avoid falling into the same trap twice. However, you got along so well with the Cancer that you might just give him a second try. After all, the two of you share some heavy karmic burdens and might need a second or third go-around to sort through them. The only advice to take is: make sure that real change has occurred before you jump back into bed with a Cancer or else your karmic lesson might become how to avoid repeat mistakes.

Gemini

It's whimsical, almost, how the Cancer tried to stuff Mercurial You into a tiny shell and keep you there, away from all the things and people you love. This failed attempt must have been rather infuriating for the poor guy, not to mention frustrating and futile. No need to worry about you, though, since Geminis have the incredible talent of withstanding nearly anything life throws at them. You may be hurt, but the Crab is splintered and charred. You may be upset, but the Crab won't come out of his shell for months. Neither of you will have much trouble finding some-one else to take up your time, but you always will be in the back of his mind, reminding him of what could have been. He is about power and control, and we all have heard how absolute power corrupts. Perhaps that is the lesson to be learned from the Crab.

Cancer

Two people of the same sign, in a significant love relationship, al-ways have the potential to bring out the best or the worst in each other. The two of you stood a better chance than most same-sign couples of being beneficial for each other. Both of you require a lot of attention and emotional support, and because you each have a tendency to hold on to exes, there's a good chance that you will either remain friends or become lovers again in the future. If that's not what you're looking for, be pleased with the idea that he will always love you, and then move on to someone more stable and interesting. You should have no problem finding someone else, but finding Mr. Right should be more important.

Leo

Your relationship with the Cancerian male was one of the strange and magical "accidents" of the zodiac. Although it's hard to imagine how the two of you got together in the first place, when looking at your astrological traits it's easy to see that there are some very important reasons that you got along so well (his devotion and jealousy, your warmth and loyalty, etc.). And there also are a few reasons why a breakup wasn't too far-fetched of a possibility, namely, his love of home and your need for society. The fact that he's a take-charge cardinal sign, and you seek control as well, didn't ease the tension any, unless you both understood your impulse to control and occasionally let the other one lead. Now that you're apart, you should be able to retain a certain respect for one another. And just because the two of you were good for one another doesn't mean that you won't be able to find someone better. You're a Leo: that's what you do.

Virgo

This is one of those sticky karmic situations that pops up in everyone's chart now and then. Both of you have some karmic debt to pay to each other, or some lesson to learn, which infuses your interactions with strong emotion, giving them the possibility of being very painful but also very worthwhile and enlightening—if you recognize the opportunities they present. Be conscious of how this breakup goes, because it probably will show you some things about yourself or your life that need changing. Each of you will miss the strange attraction and commitment you felt during this relationship, and the parting no doubt will be painful, with plenty of uncharacteristic backward glances from you. Let time heal your wounds, and then move on to other prospects while never losing sight of what you've gained from this experience.

Libra

A difficult pairing from the start. Both of you are cardinal signs, and each of you has your own idea of leadership. His romantic, sentimental nature contented you for a while; however, his emotional decision making conflicted with your own intellectual, rational approach, and his clinginess left you gasping for breath. You'll find his lack of closure and eventual desire to return to a relationship with you flattering instead of creepy, only to be let down by him once again. After dealing with his self-centeredness and manipulation a few times, you'll be willing to find your own closure to the situation. (Just remember why you left him the first time, and the second time, and make up your mind that you've had enough.) As a game player, he's met his match in you, and once you've made a decision, you'll stand by it.

Scorpio

Unlike the Crab's shell, which provides a comfy retreat from the world, your shell is made for battle. You may feel pain and betrayal, but you handle it—usually without missing a beat— whereas he's out of commission for weeks. That doesn't mean he feels more than you do; you just hide your emotions rather than your entire body. His continued halfhearted attempts at keeping you around wound your pride and probably will result in some type of verbal combat. However, if he plans on rekindling a romance with you, he'll have to prove that he intends to stay. If he can't, you'll have no problem finding other suitors.

Both of you have a tendency to get defensive and aggressive at perceived slights, so the breakup might not be easy. It would be better if you stop hiding your hurt, and he stops hiding in general, and both of you learn to respect each other as friends.

Sagittarius

For all his quirks, it didn't take you long to get bored with the Cancer. Both of you are classic jokers, but he wanted to stay at home all the time. He never wanted to go anywhere new or take off on an adventure—unless he was assured of the outcome. The worst part was his jealousy when you went off on your own. Eventually you realized that all of his eccentricities that originally delighted and fascinated you were just ordinary, boring behaviors with a twist. The fact that he liked cinnamon sprinkled on his mocha latté didn't make him an adventurer. The keyword to describe Mr. Crab is *affectation*, or maybe *posturing*. Now that you're free from the Cancerian confines, life will seem a little more vivid and a little less two-dimensional.

Capricorn

The sheer, desperate, never-ending neediness of the Cancer male left you annoyed, and when he tried to blame *you* for it, you actually could feel the bile rising in your throat. While both of you are searching for financial stability and emotional security, you'd each be a lot better off with someone who will either let you lead or be an equal partner. There were certain things that you provided for each other—you gave him emotional security while he gave you adoration and devotion—but there were far too many things left undone and unsaid. If you decide to go back to him, make sure you do it out of a sense of love rather than fear. Just because you can do better doesn't mean you need to. If he's perfect for you despite all of his imperfections, that's okay.

Aquarius

Imagine this: two people are joined at the back, one always looking toward the future and the other yearning for the past. Neither is happy, so they struggle to get to their opposite destinations, which eventually tears both of them apart. Sound familiar? Now that you're free of the Crab, you're probably thanking your lucky stars. Pining away with regret and longing is not your kind of breakup scenario. At first he was entertaining and fun, but then he became hopelessly boring and predictable. He wanted you to stay in one place when all you wanted to do was run. Not that you didn't try to stay. In fact, you tried rather hard—like you usually do. Your mental dexterity never allowed him to feel secure in a relationship with you. He always had the feeling that he'd never be able to hold on to you, and in a way, he was right. What he doesn't realize is that he could have if he'd tried harder.

Pisces

The two of you were well matched and more capable than other signs of understanding each other and providing what the other lacked. For example, he was protective where you were helpless, and you were nurturing where he wanted to be babied. A separation between the two of you is more like a test than an actual breakup, because there's a good chance that your similarities will bring you back together in the future, whether or not that's what you want right now. Without the Cancer, you'll be a little hard-pressed to find someone more suitable for you—not that it's impossible. More than any other sign in the zodiac, you understand that *nothing* is impossible. As an ex, the Cancer may be defensive and even purposely do things to hurt you, but remember that he does what he does because he still cares.

Leo

The *Leo* Ex-Boyfriend

Dates: July 23–August 23
Planet: Sun
Element: Fixed fire
Representation: Lion

Now you've done it. You've pissed off a Lion, and how are you ever going to function now that the head honcho is angry? You simply *can't*. And neither can anyone else. We might as well signal the end of the world right now, because the world cannot exist without the Sun to revolve around…*duh*. However, if you're not willing to bend and ask for a second helping of whatever the Leo did that led to the end of your love affair, then take heart. Beating him is easier than it seems—and despite popular belief, you don't have to do everything a Lion tells you to, nor do you have to stay on his good side.

Not that he knows that. Even though the two of you are separated, he's still under the impression that you need to applaud his every move and continue worshiping at his feet. If you don't, he'll be confused at first, and then angry at the assault on his pride. That is the keyword, after all: *pride*. And no matter what you do, if you're trying to maintain a shred of personal dignity in this breakup, then you'll wound his pride, because he expects nothing less from you than abject devotion—regardless of what he's done to you. He won't understand why you aren't miserable, and if you are miserable, he'll strut around and brag about it to his friends and anyone else who'll listen. Not that he doesn't have the potential to be a warmhearted, loyal man, because he does. He just doesn't know how to handle breakups. In all things in life that matter to him, there is a winner and a loser, and the fact that he isn't sure which one he is in this situation makes him a little twitchy and very defensive.

He's never going to be comfortable with your breakup unless he can convince himself that you're awaiting his heroic return. However, he doesn't want you to be desperate, even though, if you left him, he'd love to see you humiliated. He wants a challenge, and he needs you to be a prize worth attaining. Conquering your free will and independence is the most interesting game he can think of. Confused by all the do's and don'ts of the Leo? That's because he's an idealist at heart and wants everything to be just so. And you can't just expect him to leave you alone if you don't live up to who he wants you to be. Things are never that simple with the Leo. Depending on how you let him down—whether you leave him without a backward glance or you just don't live up to his ideal—he will find ways to haunt your life. He'll either ridicule you for your misdeeds and personal downfalls or attempt to lure you back into wanting him. He loves challenges, and just as a disgruntled kitten will wait around the corner to pounce on you, so too will the Lion. Just when you think you've seen the last of him, you'll feel claws scratching at your ankles.

If you're one of the "lucky" ones, then he'll assert his superiority by totally ignoring your presence or at least deeming you good enough to become his "friend" (i.e., he wants your continued adoration, but only in a format he can control). He will calmly admit that you are worthy, regally nod his head in your general direction, secretly use you to measure all of his new sexual interests against, and expect you to be there if he ever needs a fu....um, comfort. If at any time you let him down, you'll be demoted. Kinda feels like you're still in a relationship with him, doesn't it? Having to watch what you say, when you say it, and whom you say it to…Trying your hardest to avoid his temper…Stroking his ego even when you know he's wrong…It takes a very…*special* kind of woman to deal with a male Leo for any length of time, and each and every one of you deserves a Purple Heart.

What You'll Miss

He was so warm and cuddly when he wasn't trying to be a ferocious Lion. He genuinely supported you, and he encouraged you to follow your passions and progress as an individual. He helped remove the fear that kept you in line with the current trends, and he gave you the confidence to be yourself. Whenever you were in danger, he'd leap into the fray with flying teeth and claws. He was so protective.

What You Won't Miss

Ego. Attention seeking. Drama. There are so many things that you won't miss. However, because you are so used to dealing with his issues, life might seem a little too simple without him. He was the most demanding, arrogant man you've ever known. His constant putdowns left you feeling humiliated and fuming. And his inflated ego eventually led you to buy the largest needle you could find and keep it close to you just in case he took it too far one day.

How to Get Him Back
(If, for Some Reason, You Want to Know)

This is tricky because the Lion is one of those men who will want you if he can't have you and quickly dismiss you if you're too readily available. Like the Aries, he lives for his ideals, and the reality of a situation usually does nothing more than bring him down. If you're intent on getting him back in your life, you must be ready and willing to play some intense emotional games.

How to Make Sure He Stays Gone

Don't let him come back. It's that simple. The Leo is convinced that everything you do is because of him, and he's also positive that you want him back and that everything you're doing and saying is calculated to achieve that end in some way. So the only way to make sure he knows he's not wanted is to counter him every time he makes an innuendo about rekindling the flame. At first, this will make him try harder, but once his ego becomes sufficiently bruised, he'll leave you alone.

How Your Sign Will Handle the Situation

Aries

Fireworks mark the ending of this relationship, just as they did the beginning. A strong attraction for, and deep understanding of, each other brought the two of you together, but each of you had trouble finding the adoration you crave. He always was obsessing over being the star of every social event, trying to make everyone take notice of him. It was embarrassing, especially because you are hyper aware of what people really think about him. But while you were together, it was somewhat cute. Not anymore. Now that you've broken up, your egos are at war over who did what to whom and whose fault everything was and who gets to keep which friend. It's a mess, and it really will get neither of you anywhere. There are so many other men out there waiting for you to notice them and promising to be better than Mr. Leo ever was.

Taurus

Oh, Mr. Leo. You know, it's a fact of nature that Bulls don't particularly enjoy being poked and prodded. The Lion couldn't stop himself; he thought you lacked a certain "emotional vitality," and he wanted to see what it took to rouse you from your complacency. Uh-huh. Another "fact" of nature that any Lion aware of his Sun sign is more than willing to point out is that he's at the top of the food chain. He's leaving out a few key points, though, like the fact that the female lions do most of the hunting, and that they never pull down a full-grown Bull in its prime; they go only for the weak ones—and it's rare for a Taurus, even a baby one, to be weak. Well, enough of nature. Let's get back to the end of your relationship. If Mr. Leo thinks that he can strut around saying whatever he wants to about you, then he has a serious surprise in store. You might not be upfront about it, but you'll get him in the end. Even if it's just the triumph of watching his face while you move on to someone better. Bulls never trade down.

Gemini

In you, the Leo sensed a challenge. It takes someone special to convince a Gemini to settle down and stay settled down. And it's even rarer for the Twins to adore someone, which is what the Leo wants. But his real challenge was taming your independent nature and controlling you. You might have played along with it for a while, and you may have been convinced yourself that you needed to be tamed, but that damned dual nature of yours kept switching things up, and you kept changing positions. Now that you're single again, the Leo will expect you to be heartbroken and beg for his return. When you move on, he'll be hurt and confused—didn't your love mean anything? (Of course, he'll never think about how he treated you.) There's a karmic tie between you, so be prepared for some lingering tension or some lesson to be learned.

Cancer

Okay, so you can be a little timid, and you like for others to appear to have control. And Mr. Leo can be demanding and controlling. So you're expected to just lie back, dish out oodles of adoration, and let him walk all over you? Nope. You're a cardinal sign and he's merely fixed. You can change more easily than he can, but you'll direct the show, even if you have to do it passively. As an ex, he's in the midst of a power struggle: he expects you to be lost without him. After all, what would the universe do without the Sun? But you're very practical when dealing with affairs of the heart; you control whom you love and for how long you love them. You've always seen through his boasts and struts, and you know exactly how to hurt his most vulnerable spot: his pride. Luckily for him, you're more circumspect than that—unless he decides to play dirty.

Leo

When in love, two Leos easily can become the ideal King and Queen, but after the affair has ended, a royal battle breaks out among equally powerful foes. Unless one of you has a more reserved Moon sign or Ascendant, this could get really ugly, really quickly. Both of you have explosive personalities and a great deal of pride that needs to be protected. Neither of you finds it easy to admit defeat or to take responsibility for what went wrong, both of which you really wish he'd do. Be careful not to involve your friends too much or they might just become collateral damage, or worse—speed bumps as you sprint toward your prey. As an ex, especially *your* ex, he's more likely to flaunt his numerous admirers in front of you than to be honest about how afraid he is to live without you. You can't help but feel sorry for the woman who has to follow your act.

Virgo

You can be very protective of your men and even more so of the Lion, because you understand how fragile he is under all that masculine crap. He needs you, even if he won't admit it. Your understanding is the very thing that will make this breakup easier for you than for most signs. Yes, there might be some sparks here and there, some rumors started, and some conquests flaunted, but you just don't buy it. And he knows that you understand him—that's why he's so afraid of losing your respect and why he's still trying to impress you (even if he's doing anything but). You enjoyed and envied his social ease and confidence, and you'll miss the teddy-bear warmth he provided. But there are far more compatible men out there, and even though settling for comfort's sake is tempting, you would never be completely satisfied.

Libra

Your talent for flattering men, even exes, works wonders with Mr. Leo...up to a point. He'll probably never see through it; he's willing to believe every flowery compliment you pay him. It's just that when you find someone else—and you will—he'll suddenly have reason to question your loyal admiration and to doubt his ability to get you back. Not surprisingly, he'll be angry, and even though your tact will delay his outbursts, everything will come flying out now. He'll use everything he has against you: he'll start rumors, sleep with every woman within a ten-mile radius of you, pick fights, etc. It'll get old quickly, and it'll help cement the usually changeable Libran mind into making a firm decision to leave the Lion far behind. Even if he didn't do something drastic, his continual boasts and dramatic airs made him an embarrassment to date, and you're a little glad to be rid of him. The right man is still to be found; just trust your instincts.

Scorpio

This situation can easily go from bad to worse. You see, both of you are astrologically disposed to miscommunicate, and then are deeply hurt by the ensuing misunderstandings. Your quiet nature makes him think you don't care, and his boisterous gloating makes you feel unloved and replaceable. While he's a warm and charming lover, he has difficulty accepting his new outcast position as your ex, unless he can find some way to be in control of the situation. He still wants dominion over you, and he's expecting you to be heartbroken. In truth, everything does seem a little colder without his warm presence, but once he's strutted around one too many times and hurt your feelings beyond repair, you'll be playing offense.

Sagittarius

You were attracted to the Leo's warm and fun-loving personality, and you enjoyed watching him strut around admiring himself. He could appreciate a joke, as long as it didn't hurt his pride, and he was thrilled to go on adventures with you. His possessiveness and jealousy were exhausting at times, but you handled it better than you would have with another sign. He loved you, and you knew it, even when his boasting about other conquests sounded to all the world like declarations of infidelity. As an ex, you're more than capable of keeping him in line. You aren't too bothered about what he's doing, because you know better than anyone that the Leo having sex with someone doesn't have anything to do with where his heart is. There's a good chance that you'll be able to become friends after the breakup.

Capricorn

There's something about you that's unsettling to the Lion. Actually, there's a lot about you that unsettles him. He is a born social climber, as are you. However, he does his climbing through flamboyant disregard for social rules and traditions, whereas you follow the rules strictly. You were a little embarrassed by him, and he thought you were too reserved and conservative. There wasn't much that you could agree on, and neither of you gives in easily to others' demands. As an ex, he'll leave you alone (as most of your exes do). He knows you well enough to intuit when you've reached your final decision—and it's your decision that matters in the end here—and he won't risk his pride by trying to convince you to change your mind. He might talk a little crap here and there, but ultimately both of you will move on and most likely will lose contact.

Aquarius

"Opposites attract" doesn't really work here. You and the Lion believe so strongly in your own rightness that, in your opinion, anything opposite you (i.e., opposing you) is wrong. This shared trait didn't help your relationship. Also, you differed in your approaches to love and social interaction; you are more conservative and less demonstrative than is Mr. Leo. Still, his warm, exuberant nature answered one of your hidden needs—to be admired. You could appreciate him for what he was, and you didn't try to change him too much. You just weren't willing to provide the blind loyalty and admiration for which he yearns. As an ex, he's willing to exploit your weaknesses and tarnish your hard-earned reputation. He won't get too far, though, because you're smarter than he is and can come up with some interesting tidbits of gossip yourself, when the situation calls for it. Once you've finally tired of the game, there are more than a couple men waiting for your attention on the sidelines.

Pisces

You enjoyed the warm, hearty personality of the Lion more than most other signs do. You forgave him for his pride, and you admired his ability to go forth in life with such confidence. You won't stick around to find out if he gossips about you or to watch the number of women he's slept with quadruple. You know how to avoid pain when you want to, and a breakup is painful enough without the ex making things worse. Both of you easily can garner pity from others, and there will be more than enough people around to make sure you're doing all right. You'll miss his warmth, but not his need to control you, and he'll miss you very much. Because of the control he had over your life, you might be hesitant about calling it quits with him, and you might welcome the opportunity to try again. Trust in yourself and your ability to direct your own life.

Virgo

The *Virgo* Ex-Boyfriend

Dates: August 23–September 22
Planet: Mercury
Element: Mutable earth
Representation: The Virgin

Anal? They don't make a word strong enough to describe this particular characteristic of the male Virgo. To put it simply, the same quality that makes the female Virgo prudish gives this guy a sphincter so tight he has to take laxatives regularly. Not that you'd ever know it. He's an expert at hiding this physical anomaly from everyday society. You see, he's always been afraid that there's something wrong with him, so he's worked very hard at appearing normal—better than normal, actually. Occasionally, he ends up looking every bit like an alien being who has studied the art of being human. His oh-so-superior intellect gets him into trouble through over-thinking and nitpicking. (And this is where the real intellectuals will chide him for being so sub-intelligent as to cause the War of the Worlds.)

You've never been hated like the Virgo hates you. Never before has someone known every single one of your faults and weaknesses and been so willing to fling them at you with complete disregard for your feelings and intentions—and for his own shortcomings. Unless you like provoking people or are just generally masochistic, being on the wrong side of a Virgo isn't a fun experience.

When the two of you were together, he critiqued everything you did. This is how he deals with his boredom and inability to connect emotionally with people, although typically he manages to hide his suspicion that there is something deeply wrong with him. He wasn't interested in what you were, but instead in what you had the potential to become. The thought of you changing for the better made him so excited that he risked tinkling in his perfectly ironed pants—not that a Virgo would *ever* be so uncouth. He was passionately driven to see you improve, although he rarely made any significant improvements in himself.

As an ex, he's still passionate about your progress, or lack of it. He's now convinced that you have only a small chance of ever making anything of yourself. What he gloats over is not your successes but rather your continued failures, and by "gloats" I mean he's absolutely thrilled. That's why it can be dangerous to keep a slighted Virgo around—unless you think that surrounding yourself with people who wish the worst for you is exciting. On a positive note, there is a good chance that you learned a lot about yourself from this relationship and are a much stronger person because of it. Now that you've broken up, he's secretly wondering if you had a valid reason for leaving him. He's really afraid that the part of him he dislikes so much—a part that he's hyper aware of—is the reason behind the breakup. It isn't a pleasant thought, and he'll try to distract himself by preying on some unsuspecting woman.

Despite his willingness to use everything he can get his hands on against you, it's not common for a Virgo to take his hurt pride further than necessary. But just because he won't be sending you hate mail for the next twenty years doesn't mean he'll leave you completely alone either. Unless you have somehow maintained his respect, he will belittle you whenever your name comes up in conversation, and he'll hide his own fears by making sure everyone knows each of your faults. If he doesn't let out all of your secrets, he will consider himself quite merciful, and he will keep them to himself unless you do something else to piss him off.

What You'll Miss

All of his annoying qualities were really just cover-ups for his insecurities. He doesn't mean to be so callous; he's just very afraid that he's a bad person and that all of the happiness in the world is beyond his grasp and always will be. You knew, being the insightful woman that you are, that if he would just drop his defenses, he'd be able to take hold of that happiness and live a joyful life.

What You Won't Miss

Eventually, you had to come to terms with the fact that the Virgo won't ever drop his defenses. He apparently is doomed to live a life of triple-checking his taxes and teaching his significant others how to fold clothes correctly. His constant complaints and all of those changes he wanted you to make left you feeling manipulated. Now's a great time to rediscover yourself and get rid of all of those habits and thoughts he infested you with.

How to Get Him Back
(If, for Some Reason, You Want to Know)

Make all of those changes he wanted you to make. Become the woman he's always dreamed of, and convince yourself that he's the best man in the world (so you can convince him too). And be prepared when he has a new list of faults to confront you with. Convince him that you are independent and yet utterly lost without him. Challenge him without taking away his control.

How to Make Sure He Stays Gone

If a Virgo's relationship has failed, he usually won't give it a second chance, so you won't have to waste time changing your locks and phone number. However, if he is one of the rare Virgos who wants to try again, there are a few things you can do to turn him off. Refuse to acknowledge his superiority. Question his beliefs and values…and intelligence. Give up on him and let him go without a fight. Or you could take the high road and explain to him, using logic, that the two of you just don't need to be together.

How Your Sign Will Handle the Situation

Aries

He was attracted to your independence and your reluctance to back down from a fight. However, his tendency to ridicule and manipulate you upset your need for approval. Both of you demand continual acknowledgment and praise from your lovers, but how is that supposed to happen in the face of a disagreement when neither is willing to give in? Now that the two of you are separated, you'll find that dealing with the Virgo is a pain. Even if he's cautious about spreading rumors, he isn't hesitant about being openly fed up with some of the things you do. Breakups are hard enough without someone having a million logical reasons for leaving you. I assure you that there are plenty of men out there who don't keep nearly as good records as this one and are at least a little more forgiving.

Taurus

There's a good chance that your breakup won't be permanent, unless one of you did something unforgivable or you both have reached the decision that friendship would be best. The two of you have a natural understanding and compassion for one another. Both of you long for, and provide for others, stability. And you took his constant critiques better than most other signs would have. As an ex, the Virgo can be quite vocal about exactly what went wrong and whose fault he thinks it was. That's not to say that he'll lie; it's just that his version is a little unsettling, especially because he doesn't realize that it's just *his* version. While a Virgo is a good match for you, there are plenty of them out there willing to work through problems. Or you could always move on to a different sign. Having Venus on your side makes it easy to find mates.

Gemini

You have to admire the Virgo man for even attempting to leave his comfort zone and become the lover of a wayward Twin. Or perhaps instead of courage, it was a pigheaded sense that he could change you—and that you needed to be changed. Either way, you kept him on his toes, but not many Virgos are happy walking around on tiptoe. It reminds them of walking on eggshells, and they're too blunt to enjoy doing that either. However, his initial bravery didn't exactly transfer over to the rest of the affair. After the deal was sealed, it suddenly became open season on all of your faults. That might turn some women into little lumps of workable, manageable clay, but you know for a fact that there are other fish in the sea. Now that you're single, go find one. Have fun. You've nothing to fear from a little Virgo meanness.

Cancer

This is one of those karmic entanglements that can define a person. All pressure aside, the two of you had a certain affinity for each other. The one problem you may have run into stems from the fact that you are a cardinal sign and the Virgo male is merely mutable. Although sometimes you genuinely like direction, you have a deep dislike for being controlled, and you eventually balked at the Virgo's critiques. You like having things in their place, but you know that disorder sometimes is indicative of comfort, and you didn't like having your shoes sanitized every time you walked through the door. Don't get caught up in past mistakes; move on and make a better choice next time. Maybe a Pisces or Taurus will come along and provide the stability and acceptance you crave. Now that you're free to find your perfect mate, don't settle for less.

Leo

The Virgo never knew what happened to him. You came into his nice, tidy life and promptly turned everything inside out, backwards, and slightly to the left. His meticulous nitpicking, his many complaints, and his emotional aloofness both bored you and made you wonder if there really was something wrong. There was. It's called a difference of personalities. If he thinks he's going to get the upper hand now that the two of you are separated, he's asking for some serious trouble. Luckily for him, Leos aren't really inclined to start wars with their exes; however, they aren't quietly complacent in their exile either. Being free means that you're now able to explore all of those people and places you had to deprive yourself of before. The Virgo may sling insults at you now and then, but you'll quickly outdistance him.

Virgo

Any time two people of the same sign come together and then split up, the question is raised about projection. Did you see your faults in your partner, and could you not stand it, blaming the other person for them? Did your partner subconsciously remind you too much of yourself? Shouldn't you embrace all your qualities rather than run from them? If you're having any trouble sleeping, think about these questions and eventually they'll wear you out...or drive you crazy. Hopefully, both of you were able to come to terms with your issues and maintain respect for each other throughout the breakup. That would be the ideal, and both of you love ideals. However, if you happened to step on each other's toes, and you weren't able to come to a mutual understanding about your differing opinions, then there's hope in the fact that both of you can easily move on if you really want to. If not, there'll be a lot of backward glances and unanswered questions.

Libra

There is a general misconception that female Librans are compliant women who gently persuade people to do what they want them to. According to many astrologers, they will let men walk all over them, which is true—up to a point. And no one is as skilled at finding that point as a Virgo. In truth, you know how to control every situation you're in, and you aren't sure how to live without that control. Even though you know how to stand up for yourself, you always question whether you should change for your partner, and Mr. Virgo demands a lot of changes. The

Virgo isn't easily charmed by your wit, and he doesn't buy all of your compliments and helplessness either. As an ex, his sharp insights into your problems and personality are uncomfortable, and you'd rather be far away from him. You'll miss his guidance, but there are men out there who will appreciate you for who you are rather than who you could be.

Scorpio

The two of you had a problem with the basics: he basically wanted to mold you into someone else, and, as a water sign, you didn't mold easily—and you basically resented anyone who tried to make you do so (unless you were frozen, and then you weren't really molded but, more technically, were *carved*). As exes, each of you is quite critical of the other, and neither will easily admit that it's because you're hurt. There's a lot more going on than what you're currently aware of. The ties are stronger and the root of the problem is deeper than would be the case with most other signs. This is one of those lessons that's better learned at once instead of dealing with it over and over again. So pay attention. There's someone else out there who's better suited for you, but that doesn't mean you get to skip this lesson.

Sagittarius

What, oh what, can a Sagittarius woman do with a Virgo lover? I have no idea. He was so damned judgmental and opinionated, and *blind*. He was great at straightening you out, but you enjoy being a little bent. He was good at correcting your flaws, but you are wise enough to know that flaws to some people are virtues to others. He could intuit your moods, but you're very independent, and having a critical observer telling you what you felt didn't go over well after a while. Now that you've broken up, little has changed except that he's telling others about your flaws too—not that he was too quiet about them before. Oh well, you're a busy woman who has a million better things to concentrate on. He'll leave you alone, and you'll move on quickly.

Capricorn

The two of you were mostly compatible. Both of you know how important physical things (such as money and comfort) are, and how to attain them. However, you also share a tendency to critique each other, and though it took a while for that to become destructive, it eventually did. Both of you brought out the best and the worst in each other, and if you want to give your relationship a second chance, I have two bits of advice: open up the lines of communication, and stop being so hard on each other. Even if you decide that you really are finished, the breakup most likely will be quiet and calm, with neither of you letting the other know just how affected you really are. Maybe a friendship can be built on this shaky foundation, or maybe not. Either way, there are other men out there with their eyes on you, and one is bound to be more accepting than the Virgo was.

Aquarius

His critical quips and dirty looks triggered your need for approval and desire to have others look up to you. How can you go around teaching others how to lead their lives, and living your own life impeccably, when some man is following you around, correcting your grammar and carrying a bottle of stain remover in case you spill your coffee? Who's supposed to take you seriously? It would have been okay if he had been willing to work behind the scenes and let you have the spotlight, but no, that would have damaged his pride. In short, there were a lot of problems. However, now that you're apart, you'll find that things are pretty much irrevocably over, and both of you are fine with it. What you might not be fine with is how the Virgin's critiques didn't end with your relationship; but don't worry, everyone knows what he's like. Now you're free to find someone more intellectual and entertaining, someone who acknowledges your positive qualities.

Pisces

In cases of opposites attract, there are two possibilities: either you will supply what the other is lacking or you will pull each other apart. He provided structure and stability, which many people believe you lack; however, his rigidity didn't allow you the freedom you need. So, logically, you retreated within yourself—the only retreat he has no control over—and this infuriated him, driving you even further away. It was a vicious cycle, and now that it has stopped, you will be a little relieved—and a little upset. Opposites hold a strange fascination for one another. Even though under perfect conditions the two of you would be able to remain friends or even reunite as lovers, both of you are too open to hurt, and by the time the chance comes along, you might not feel like taking it.

Libra

The *Libra* Ex-Boyfriend

Dates: September 23–October 23
Planet: Venus
Element: Cardinal air
Representation: The Scales

As idealistic as some other zodiac signs, the Libran expects to find the perfect *romance* whereas other signs might expect to find the perfect *partner.* The male Libran longs to be carried away by a dramatic affair, but has no idea how to make the romance last and will cause problems in the relationship just to make things interesting when he gets bored. This, and his indecisiveness, are the main reasons that male Librans tend to cheat more than any sign in the zodiac. He knows how to spot a problem from a mile away, but has no idea how to solve it and no faith in being patient. (After all, why be patient when it just means that you'll be too old and ugly to have fun once you've finally found out you've made a mistake by sticking around, hoping for things to get better?)

As an ex, the Libran will be more than happy to turn all of your friends against you. If this means that he'll have to sleep with half of New York and start his own talk show, then he'll obligingly make the sacrifice if it means isolating you. Why would he want you isolated? There are a few reasons. To prove a point: Libra = the World; therefore, no Libra = no World. And from an evolutionary point of view, if you and he are the last people in the world, then you are more likely to focus your attention on him again. He has another, more vulnerable reason for wanting everyone on his side: he's afraid he's made a mistake. And because he is such a socio…social person, his anxiety can be put to rest only if the opinions of everyone else support what he's done. There's nothing like a closed door or lost opportunity to make a Libran hyperventilate and send him into a minor catatonic state in which he cannot do anything for fear of accidentally making a mistake. And in the realm of human society, few doors get slammed as loudly as those that are closed in a breakup.

It takes the poor Libran a while to get over a breakup—not because he was actually emotionally involved with the person, but because the breakup brought all of his negative traits into sharp relief, stripping him of the usual masks he hides behind. Thinking that there might be someone out there who knows him very well and still doesn't want to be with him—still doesn't find him good enough—isn't one of those happy thoughts that makes a person fly, even with a bucketful of fairy dust. He'll also get a little paranoid, wondering what you're doing now that you're free (the Libran isn't *that* far from the Scorpio in the zodiac, and Scorpio is *the* sign of the stalker)...wondering if you're telling anyone about his secrets, if you're making fun of him. So he'll overreact if he hears that you're hanging out with his best friend or that you've told his favorite bartender that he snores in his sleep. He'll think you've declared war, and that gives him the right to attack you. This is one of the biggest reasons for him to make sure you're isolated, as isolated people can't spread rumors.

The male Libran (and, to be fair, the female one as well) is addicted to attention. Even when in a crowded room where everyone is paired up in private conversation, there is a part of the

Libran that secretly insists that every female in the room wants to be with him, and every male in the room is horribly jealous. But he will never admit this, and he is so skilled at manipulating people and situations that most people would never guess he does this. He's also addicted to control, and everything he does and says is calculated to provide him with more of it. As an ex, he'll be even more desperate than usual for control, and his grasping and manipulations will be worse because of it. It's up to you to decide whether you'll let him think he still has some or you'll leave little doubt about his new position in your life.

What You'll Miss

A romance with a male Libran often feels like an otherworldly experience. Everything is perfect. He looks deep in your eyes and says all the right things. He puts up just enough of a fight for you to think that he's struggling to accept the incredible amount of love he has for you (when in actuality he's struggling with the concept of commitment). He convinces you that you alone have his heart and that, in you, he's finally found his perfect match.

What You Won't Miss

The roving eyes. The manipulation. The utter lies. Just because he made you feel like you were the only girl able to tame his wicked heart doesn't mean you really were. All of the inner struggles were struggles between his sense of fairness and his need to experience a romantic connection to every woman on the planet—or at least the attractive ones. He got bored easily, and all the problems he created when he needed a little more excitement did some serious damage to your sense of security.

How to Get Him Back
(If, for Some Reason, You Want to Know)

Present a logical argument—without sounding desperate or clingy —as to how neither of you tried hard enough during the last go-around, and include all of the things you, personally, plan on improving. Don't blame him at all for the breakup, but do blame him for not wanting to try again, and make sure you pump up his ego while you're at it. If that doesn't work, let him know how desperately you are wanted by his rivals. (Librans always have rivals, because it makes their lives more dramatic and their actions more enviable.)

How to Make Sure He Stays Gone

There are two circumstances under which a Libran will let you go: either he decides that you no longer are worth keeping around, or you don't give him a choice. A Libran can be strung along just as easily as he can keep you dangling. With a mixture of charm and cruelty, you can pretend to have a continued interest in him, making promises both you and he know you have no intention of keeping, and then wait until he's emotionally exhausted enough to stop caring about whether you'll come back to him. Or you can go about it the healthy way and let him know that you have no intention of rekindling the flame.

How Your Sign Will Handle the Situation

Aries

Despite the Libran's ability to be extremely affectionate and appear utterly loyal, you always got a funny feeling whenever another female was around. You knew instinctively that he always was on the lookout for another lover, and because of that you weren't able to fully relax around him. Now that you aren't together anymore, don't be surprised when he finds a new lover or three—and he shouldn't be surprised when you easily find someone new too. Even though both of you were highly attract-ed to each other, better mates do exist. The breakup will feel a little strange, because both of you hope the other will fix your faults and that happily ever after might exist somewhere in the future. In some cases, people can change and a romance can be rekindled, but in most you'd be better off finding someone else to lavish your affection on than the bottomless-Libran-pit.

Taurus

Although there simply is no way for the Libran to provide you with the security you desire, you still found his company en-joyable and entertaining. Because you share the planet Venus with your Sun signs, you and Mr. Taurus have a certain affinity for one another and a certain understanding about why you do what you do. However, his unpredictable and aloof nature, his "need" for variety in the bedroom, and his logical arguments against monogamy sent you into fits of depression and anger (which is only pushed-down, "depressed" anger). You want to feel loved, and you expend so much energy helping everyone else that you deserve better than how he treated you. Luckily, you're also attractive, and there already is someone else who has his eye on you. As an ex, the Libran will be upset when you move on, but who cares? He's an ex, isn't he?

Gemini

The four of you (because you both are a dual sign, of course) were, for the most part, well matched. A breakup between such compatible people often is confusing for outsiders who aren't aware of how difficult it is to keep such a crowd in line. There are completely logical and rational reasons for which you might decide to call it quits and find someone different. And you both are hard to predict anyway, so there's no telling exactly what drove you apart. However, the separation is easier than it could have been, because one or both of you is adamant about it— you'd have to be or else it never would have happened. And once either of you makes such a decision, you stand solidly behind it, at least for now. There might be a few catty remarks now and then, or maybe a couple of rumors, but nothing too horrible. Any residual pain after the breakup has mostly to do with regret over the loss of what could have become the Great Romance.

Cancer

Oh, the damage that this supposedly thoughtful and caring man did to you! He was so arrogant and indecisive, and so self-centered. What he didn't expect from such a charming and quiet woman like you was the passion and drive that come from your cardinal nature. You saw through his manipulations and arguments, even if you weren't exactly sure what to do about them. As an ex, you'll still be able to see through his charming exterior, and you're woman enough, and watery enough, to be hurt by his attempts to control you. Is he really trying to control you? Yes. Undoubtedly. And one of the most hurtful things he does is attempt to string you along. No matter what his intentions, he can't keep you from figuring out that better, more compatible men exist, and you have everything it takes to get into a much healthier relationship.

Leo

A good relationship needs a stable foundation. We all remember our mothers telling us this, right? Well, the two of you had your work cut out for you because he's a born flirt and you're a very possessive woman. Your jealousy was triggered so often that you almost forgot what it's like to feel secure. Someone more adoring and loyal would be a much better mate for you, and now that you're suddenly single, you can find Mr. Perfect. The Libran will use all his charms to stay on good terms with you, as long as you don't step on his ego too often. There's a warmth between you that, when carefully flamed, can provide a good foundation for friendship. He won't be happy to see you with someone else; he's a little possessive too, you know.

Virgo

Did someone call him charming? A good catch? Ha! They're free to try, because you've been there and done that, and you found him wanting. A Virgo woman will do just about anything she can for her lover; however, you were stretched to the limit by this flirtatious and manipulative man. You tried, though. Surprisingly enough, it wasn't his cheating that forced you to end things (because this relationship won't ever really be over until *you* end it), but instead it was his lack of consideration, his lack of care. You loved him—you really did. But you've had enough, and lately other men have been knocking at your door. Remember, most Libran males come back to their exes looking for a second chance and a little comfort from the familiar. That's why it'll have to be you who makes the decision to leave if you want the separation to be permanent.

Libra

Because you're so painfully aware of your own downfalls and issues, you knew what to expect before you even got together with the Libran. You knew he'd flirt, manipulate, and possibly even lie. You knew there'd be a power struggle and that playing fair was going to be a challenge. And now that you're single again, and the man you once knew so intimately is suddenly little more than a stranger, you still know what to expect from him. Both of you will try to remain friends, and both of you will hurt each other when you each find someone new. Librans are sentimental people, and the memories that haunt you are bittersweet. But with time, they'll become less painful and more nostalgic, and eventually he'll just become a measuring stick for how far you've come in your life.

Scorpio

If the Libran pulled any of his usual tricks either during or after your relationship, then he'd better watch his back. And if he expects to string you along with empty promises, he'd better hire himself a bodyguard. You don't buy the Libran's crap; you see right through his charm and charisma, and you have no problem understanding what he wants from you. While you were together, he was outwardly hurt and resentful of your skillful, probing questions regarding his character—he swore that you were questioning his integrity. The truth is, you knew what you were talking about, and no Libran likes being unmasked so easily. After being separated for a while, he'll come to terms with you seeing other men, and he'll eventually stop trying to charm you into remaining romantically interested in him. Until then, he should be prepared to be in your line of fire if he can't behave himself.

Sagittarius

For once, the male Libran has met a woman who challenges him in very important ways: first, she's more in need of freedom than he is; and second, she isn't as easy to charm into doing everything his way as most other women have been. The breakup will be clean and simple, if you want it to be, because all you have to do is walk away. Clean and simple, yes, but I can't guarantee you that it will be pain-free. There's just something about that man that tugs at you. During a breakup, you both have a tendency to avoid open conflict and instead try to invoke memories and be seductive in order to keep the hold you have over your ex. The games are entertaining, and the challenge is exciting in a way, but eventually everything will settle down and each of you will move on.

Capricorn

Flippant, arrogant, controlling, disloyal, lying, cheating…the list could go on forever about what exactly is wrong with your Libran ex. And you're right, he is all of those things, and a few more. He simply wasn't what you needed him to be, and you resent that he was able to pretend for so long. In fact, you feel a little manipulated. Normally you don't rush into things, and you like to know what you're getting yourself into, but he didn't play fair. He knew what you were looking for, and it's like he put on the costume of your Ideal Mate, and as soon as you committed, he changed. So much for a guy who continually harps about fairness and justice, huh? Now that you're free, you'll have to regain your composure just a bit, think about what exactly it is that you want from the male species, and then go out and find it. You've got what it takes to be loved for who you really are and not who you could be.

Aquarius

Even though there are a lot of astrologers who claim that you two are nearly perfect for each other, you know differently. Yes, you can have a reasonable conversation, and both of you are intelligent, but he was just so…vain and self-absorbed. He manipulated you and eventually demanded to be in charge, and you just didn't have enough faith in him to let him. Who can really blame you? Things aren't simple or quiet after your breakup either. For some reason, you pose a threat to each other, and unless one of you finally is declared either generally superior or the victor in the situation, then the problems will continue. It would be much better if you just moved on and used your bright intellect for something more productive, like discovering a cure for cancer.

Pisces

When the Libran's scales are heavily unbalanced, and your ocean is dark and gloomy, the two of you are a recipe for disaster. Unless one of you has a Virgo, Taurus, or otherwise rigid sign in your natal chart, the two of you could easily fall into severe mutual depression or even substance abuse. Because neither of you is an extremely decisive individual, there's a chance that the bad times went on for too long before a decision was made to break things off. Not that everything has to be, or necessarily was, bad. Considering how highly creative and tactful both of you are, there was a chance that the relationship could have turned out beautifully. Now, because of those same qualities, the breakup won't be too difficult. Just watch out for the Libran's lies.

Scorpio

The *Scorpio* Ex-Boyfriend

Dates: October 24–November 22
Planet: Pluto
Element: Fixed water
Representation: Scorpion

When you and Mr. Scorpion were still deeply in love and there was no real reason to feel uncertain about your relationship, you nonetheless had an inkling that something wasn't quite right. His laughter never reached his troubled eyes, his voice held an urgency you couldn't define, and when your love turned physical, there was a desperate quality to it, as though he was afraid he'd never touch you again. Sometimes he clung to you, and sometimes he would toss you aside without a second glance. Sometimes he accused you of betraying him, calling you names and spreading rumors, and sometimes he begged you to forgive him. He'd ignore you, and the next moment he would act as if he was your long-lost Siamese twin. There wasn't a method to his madness; the Scorpion was just practicing survival maneuvers in an attempt at self-preservation. Few people are aware of just how deeply Scorpios feel: their sensitivity is the secret trigger to their poisonous vengefulness. When you love so hard, any pain you experience feels eternal and all-encompassing. Most people are quick to learn how to defend against experiencing that kind of intense pain again. The Scorpion can't entirely shut himself off from love, but he puts up a lot of walls in an attempt to block out the pain.

From the moment you met him, there was a seductive feeling of danger that positively oozed from both ends of this watery Scorpion, although a harsh tongue and heavy boots usually take the place of pincers and stingers in the human version of this sign. When you still were trying to extract every bit of information you could get from your friends about this mysterious man, you found out that he didn't have a reputation for being the nicest guy you'd ever want to meet (a rumor confirmed while you were dating), so don't be surprised when he doesn't turn out to be the sweetest—or sanest—ex in the world either.

When Scorpios make the transition from treasured lover to annoying ex, they tend to get lost somewhere in the hubbub. By "get lost," I don't mean they'll accept the situation and give you a farewell kiss on the cheek and a letter of recommendation for your new love interest right before turning around and never seeing you again (although that's exactly what the Scorpio hopes he'll be able to do). What I mean is that he doesn't know how to give his heart to someone and then complacently fit it back into his chest when it's thrown back at him with "return to sender" written all over it. He'll struggle between approaching the situation with a reserved and reasonable air, and driving by your house in the middle of the night to make sure you're alone (with a basketful of rotten eggs and a bouquet of roses in the passenger seat just in case he either feels the urge for vengeance or sees a chance to beg you to come back).

You see, when a Scorpion falls in love, his ruling planet (Pluto) takes over and everything becomes a life-or-death struggle—incredibly dark, romantic, and tragic. The breakup is just another part of that struggle; it's the closing act. He truly feels, at the close, that you are the only one who has ever mattered—or ever will matter—to him. How is he ever to come to grips with that loss? His two choices are: win you back, or teach you a lesson. It all depends on the Scorpio and how secure he is. When you were with him, you were forced to deal with these contradictions, and you never knew exactly which one you'd have to face on any given day. The breakup isn't any different. Eventually he will wear himself out, or else be persuaded by the local law enforcement to cease his harassment.

What You'll Miss

The ambition that drives him to be the best in all he does gave you pride in your man and ensured both his and your financial security. With his intensity and loyalty, he could make you feel desired and cherished. He took care of you with the dedication of a soul mate and beat himself up if he ever let you down. He also was very intelligent, and the two of you had some pretty amazing conversations.

What You Won't Miss

Let's just say that the stalking didn't exactly begin *after* you broke up. In truth, it had been going on for a while. Many women in today's liberated society have this curious desire without which they can't seem to be happy in a relationship: the desire to feel like they have a free choice in the matter of whether or not they will stay in a relationship. The Scorpio secretly understood that you had a choice—that's what scared him the most.

How to Get Him Back
(If, for Some Reason, You Want to Know)

This is hard. It really depends on how the two of you ended things. If you cheated—and it doesn't really matter how badly he thinks he wants you back—the trust has been destroyed and he'll never be able to relax in a relationship with you. If the two of you parted company maturely, without any blame on either side, then there's a good chance that somewhere down the road, if you're still a respectable person, he'll be interested in trying again. It all depends on whether he can still trust you. If he can, you have a better chance of getting him to come back. If he can't, then things won't last long even if he does return.

How to Make Sure He Stays Gone

Break his trust. Start seeing someone new, preferably someone he was always afraid you were interested in anyway. If he starts stalking you, leave the blinds open and have wild sex with his best friend. Or, if you're afraid of inciting his vengeance, make it perfectly clear to him that you respect him, like him, and think he's great, but you don't think anything romantic between you would work right now, and give him some concrete, no-fault reasons.

How Your Sign Will Handle the Situation

Aries

Caught off-guard by your passion, the Scorpio tried to temper your personality into something that complemented his own cold manner. Your independence triggered his jealousy, and he eventually stooped to following you around to make sure you weren't doing anything he didn't approve of. For you, things became downright claustrophobic. However, your own sense of loyalty is strong, and you were better able than most signs to calm his suspicions and talk him into letting you have some space. Until now. Now he *knows* you're doing something he doesn't like, and you aren't about to modify your life to satisfy an ex. He'll just have to get used to you doing what you want to, and if he doesn't like it, too bad. He still might follow you for a while, but he'll get bored…eventually. Right?

Taurus

There was something about him that fascinated you, and there was something sensual about you that satisfied his deep need to be connected to another soul. In a way, you two did well together. He desperately needed stability, and you were more than capable of providing it for him. However, his emotional swings and his jealousy and vengefulness left you feeling as though your integrity had been questioned. You were forced to scramble to find new ways to show him you cared, as he called into question everything you'd done previously. Now that you're apart, you still feel misunderstood by him, and you wonder if things would have gone differently if you'd tried harder. Don't trouble yourself so much. Chances are you did everything you could think of. Now's your chance to take care of yourself and find someone who'll appreciate all your efforts.

Gemini

Even though he was extremely manipulative emotionally, and sometimes it even felt as though he had trapped you into being with him, you are the one who holds all of the cards. A Scorpio loves intensely, and Pluto, his ruler, often makes his relationships seem like life-or-death experiences. However, your own ruler,

Mercury, gives you a certain detachment from what's going on around you. In other words, you can leave him more easily than he can leave you. And once you're separated, you'll move on more quickly than he will. He doesn't like it. He questions whether you ever really loved him, whether you cheated on him before your relationship ended, and whether you miss him the way he misses you. Scorpios are very intense people. Everything they do is tinged with drama, so you can expect him to be a little strange.

Cancer

Well, you made a good pair while it lasted. Sure, there might have been small idiosyncrasies and misunderstandings that made things difficult, but overall your personalities meshed well. Few people can withstand a Scorpion's assault better than a Cancer (who can retreat into her protective shell). Now that the relationship is over and both of you are feeling unsettled and hurt, things still will go better than they would with most other signs. During your time together, the Scorpio felt very protective of you, and he won't abruptly stop now, even though he might wish he could. He still might insult you or follow you around, because he still cares about you and misses you. But this is a time for you to think about what *you* want—and go after it.

Leo

There is a huge chance that someone—one of you or possibly even an innocent bystander—will get hurt when this pairing calls it quits. You're a little too confident of yourself and your reasons behind your actions to escape hurting the Scorpion's pride and, therefore, incurring his wrath. He isn't happy about your willingness to move on, and the line of suitors that has been waiting for you to become single again makes his stomach lurch with jealousy. You won't mind that much if he wants to follow you around (after all, it gives you a rapt audience), but only up to a point. And when he crosses that point, you'll let him know. You aren't afraid of his harsh words, even if some of them ring true. (The Scorpio is skilled in the art of vengeance, you know.) You understand that they're just a sign that he still has feelings for you.

Virgo

You may know intuitively that when a Scorpion decides to get into a relationship and allows a woman to get past the defenses he's built up over the years, he expects the relationship to be eternal. If your instincts and perceptions have gotten you that far, then they also might have told you that if things don't work out the way Mr. Scorpio expects, he won't be happy. In fact, he'll be downright miserable. *And* angry. All right, you know that much. So what? He has nothing in his arsenal of too-true insults that you don't already know about yourself, and you know a few choice things about his pitfalls too, if he's so willing to go down that road. You're the one woman in the zodiac who's more than capable of besting a Scorpio. Maybe, hopefully, he intuits that. This is one of those karmic things, though, and there's a lesson somewhere in it that you need to learn.

Libra

There isn't a cardinal sign in the zodiac who is capable of sitting back demurely and allowing someone to take full, uncompromising control of her life (not even the soft-spoken Cancer can do it). Yes, you're tactful, and an expert at the art of letting others think they're getting the best of you. (If you're a Libran who isn't conscious you're doing this, then you're frequently surprised by people who think they have the upper hand.) But the Scorpion won't fall for the charade, and he won't settle for his control over you being a façade. He has to have *real* control, because without it he leaves himself open to being taken advantage of, and that is a fate synonymous with death, according to the Pluto-ruled man. In fact, the ending of your relationship is further proof to him that if he lets others dictate his fate, he'll come to emotional and egotistical ruin. Things may never be calm between you again.

Scorpio

Astrologers often have said that the only person able to withstand the Scorpion's sting is another Scorpion—and neither Scorpion is likely to stop stinging until one of them is dead, at least metaphorically speaking. That doesn't make things all nice and easy, does it? Together, you were all intensity and passion and drama. Now that you're separated, the absence of all that angst is what's painful. Each of you has a point to make, but neither is willing to listen to the other. Behind your stoicism, you both have a penchant for drama, and this can turn into a highly dramatic situation. Eventually, the conflict will get old, and you'll be able to move on to someone less volatile. But even that small move can instigate a new jealous fit of rage, causing the cycle to start yet again. One of you will need to end the battle definitively in order for both of you to move on.

Sagittarius

The relationship was fun at least some of the time, as both of you tend to be outgoing in different ways. Your tactlessness tended to offend him, and his retaliation sent you into either bouts of laughter or silent disapproval after a sharp reproach. You love your independence, and he couldn't stand not knowing exactly which aisle of the grocery store you were in when he called your cell phone, and who you were with, and what you were buying, and who had just called you, and where you were going next, and what you were thinking, and whether you thought your friend's boyfriend was cute, and why you were flirting with the bag boy…It drove you nuts. Imagine how difficult it must be to *be* him if just being with him was so tiring. Now that you can move on, you will…easily. And if the Scorpio gets to be too much, you'll stop him.

Capricorn

The calm stability you give to those you love made it easy for the Scorpio to let you take at least some control of the relationship. Your loyalty eased his fear of rejection and betrayal. Your slow advancement into important relationships equaled his own. However, his emotional baggage weighed you down. He set you up to pay for everything that any woman had ever done that hurt him. It wasn't easy being a martyr on that cross. After the separation, both of you will suffer from severe disappointment and neither of you will find relief in swapping accusations. You will nurse your pain quietly, and your stolid personality will make it difficult for him to find anything to hurt you with—not that he won't try. This pairing rings with karmic obligation. Somewhere in the midst of the turmoil is a lesson or debt that must be dealt with if you are to grow. Maybe just moving on is enough. There are far more compatible men out there.

Aquarius

It's hard to believe that the two of you could ever stand each other long enough to form a relationship. Maybe all the difficulties and struggles brought you closer, but if that was the case, they led to your demise as well. The differences of personalities are where things really got tough. He was emotional, and you were intellectual, and neither of you knew exactly when to compromise. His clinginess was a good excuse for the breakup, and his stings of vengeance roused your own imposing temper: even after the breakup he will need to be careful about how far he takes his insults. In fact, your confidence helps make the breakup permanent and keeps the Scorpio from following you around too closely. It will simply get to the point where he doesn't want to know what you're up to. Not that you're doing anything wrong; you just have your own life to lead.

Pisces

Perhaps you don't want to hear this, and maybe you'll disagree, but the two of you were highly compatible. Each of you had a tendency to provide what the other sorely needed. The qualities in each of you that other signs find frustrating or mysterious were what endeared you to each other. It was almost as if the two of you spoke your very own language. However, things haven't turned out well, and you are either finished for good or taking a meaningful break. Just because, according to Sun sign astrology, you were meant to be together doesn't mean that there isn't someone out there better suited for you as an individual. As an ex, the Scorpio is less likely to sting you than if you were another sign; however, you usually move on more quickly than he does, and his mind will be full of accusations and assumptions once you do.

Sagittarius

The *Sagittarius* Ex-Boyfriend

Dates: November 23–December 21
Planet: Jupiter
Element: Mutable fire
Representation: Centaur, also the Archer

Don't expect him to sit around, mourning the loss of you and daydreaming about when you'll come back. Okay, he might daydream about it a little, but he won't be sitting around doing it. He'll be doing it while doing it. To be frank, if he's wondering about your return, or missing you at all, he'll be doing it while…um…pumping away. You see, sexual release clears his mind. No, really. And, there's a very good chance he was…clearing his mind…with other women long before he officially called it quits with you. If you ever find out about his immoral extracurricular activities, and if you're brave enough to ask him why he did what he did, he'll probably cite boredom, or curiosity, or some other equally infuriating non-reason—like it being the best way for him to find out if he truly loved you.

It's almost as if he doesn't realize he's done anything wrong. And actually, he probably doesn't realize it, especially now that the two of you are separated. If you try to argue with him about why he should care that you're hurt, he'll just launch in to an intellectual diatribe about the downside of monogamy and end with a monologue about how it isn't his fault you're hurt—it's yours, for letting yourself feel hurt. After all, no one can *make* you feel anything. If he's contrite, it usually isn't because he feels sorry for betraying you, but rather because he's either sorry that it wasn't as fun as he'd thought it would be or else he's sorry about the consequences.

If, and this is a really big "if," you happened to find the rare Sagittarian who honestly never cheated on you or never even really thought of cheating, then something must have been haywire in his birth chart. Although he may never have crossed the line with another woman while he was with you, even the most honorable Sags out there flirt. They're like Geminis in that they simply cannot seem to stop themselves (but it wouldn't hurt if they tried every now and then). When it's your mom he's flirting with, it's cute, but when it's your best friend, the man needs to pick up a handbook of psychological phrases and look up the term *boundaries*. As an ex, these simple flirtations can take on a whole different meaning and set off some wild and painful thoughts about betrayal and jealousy.

When you were together, the Sag could be a true gentleman, not to mention entertaining company. He had plenty to say about everything, and his intelligence and quick wit made for lively conversation. He didn't always know what to say, and he wasn't very tactful, but his social foibles gave him a boyish charm and usually were easily forgiven, unless you could see through his act. While he prides himself on being able to take care of his partners, he's really very insensitive when dealing with any issues or fears that his women have. The occasional Sag will seem to be entranced by a woman with heavy baggage, and unable to get away from dramatic relationships, but most of them would rather date a woman without any defenses, doubts, or problems of any kind. They all are searching for an ideal, as many people are, but they are so confident in their ability to attract anyone they want that they find it hard to "settle" for someone less than perfect. And when difficulties start popping up in a relationship—as happens in all relationships—they would rather cut and run than try to work things out.

Despite all the Sag's issues, women often find it difficult to let this man go. He's an irresistible challenge. However, he's not necessarily a great prize. Sometimes we're better off not having what we crave. Like Garth Brooks sang, "Thank God for unanswered prayers." The rare Sag who is able to rise above his sign is far more worthy than his brethren; he's also not so intent on leaving or getting his own way.

What You'll Miss

The Centaur was one helluva fun guy. He had so many hobbies and interests, and he loved conversing about the world and people. He loved to travel and see new places, which gave him an air of the adventurer. He was sweetly naïve and had a tendency to find intriguing and overlooked aspects of even the most mundane things. He knew how to act like a gentleman and take care of his date with a sophisticated air, but he also was perfectly able to be rough when he wanted to—all depending on his mood.

What You Won't Miss

The simple fact is that it was hard to tell if you were the only woman he was spending time with. Even though he thought he had given you lots of hints about what would happen, he still managed to catch you by surprise…and they weren't always good surprises. Yes, he was adventurous and fun, but a lot of the time he preferred to go off on an adventure without you. He was quiet when he disliked something, which made compromises hard and eventually made you question the stability of the relationship. It never seemed to be you that he loved, but only what you represented to him.

How to Get Him Back
(If, for Some Reason, You Want to Know)

Hmm. This is difficult. Once a Sag really leaves, he has kind of steeled himself against any attempt you might make to get him back. (He also has protected himself from fully feeling the pain of the breakup.) The best way to get him back is to show him that you're still interesting and fun, and that he won't be able to find anyone new who can top what you have to offer. He loves chasing the unattainable, just to prove to himself that it's within his grasp if he really wanted it. Be confident and independent. Don't cling, but don't let him go too far.

How to Make Sure He Stays Gone

Cling to him, beg him to return, and never give him a moment's rest. Follow him and interrupt his fun activities. Tell him that you want to have his baby, that you want the two of you (the three of you, if you include the baby) to settle down for good. In other words, present him with a set of rusty shackles attached to a kitchen (thank you women's lib), jiggle them around a bit so he can hear the clanking of the chains, let him know that you have yet to find a key, and then watch him run away like a scared bunny.

How Your Sign Will Handle the Situation

Aries

Something that neither of you probably wants to hear right now is how compatible you were, and that you understood each other on a deeper level than most people get to, and loved with the sort of passion created only when two fire signs join together. You know better than anyone else why such a wonderful relationship fell apart. The two of you are notorious for clinging to ideals (even if you're realists, you're still idealistic realists) and not giving an inch when you think you're right. The Sag was so independent and, for some reason, untrustworthy that you felt you had to worry about where he was at all times. He simply couldn't commit the way you needed him to, and you found it hard to put your heart on the line for someone who was never really there. Now that he's really not there, you'll be free to find someone more loyal. Just try not to be concerned with what Mr. Sag is doing now.

Taurus

For a person who loves stability, you certainly took a walk on the wild side when you made the decision to become romantically involved with a Centaur. True, some Bulls have a wild streak, but this relationship didn't make you feel secure. In fact, it more likely made you feel paranoid. You see, a Taurus woman is more than capable of providing her paramours with love, attention, good food, and generally anything that makes a man feel well cared for. But you could never shake the feeling that your Sag was dissatisfied, and you had no idea what to do about it. It wasn't you; it was the fact that the Sag is on an eternal search for…something. He doesn't even know exactly what he's looking for, so how could you be expected to provide it? Remember, you are more than capable of making a man feel wanted and content, and there are plenty of men looking for that feeling. And for you.

Gemini

Are you certain the two of you had a relationship? I don't mean to doubt the love you shared, but the two of you are so…independent and flighty that I doubt either of you was home long enough to cement an actual relationship. Maybe you learned to travel together, and your shared adventures drew you closer. Maybe you loved the freedom, and understood each other's need for it. But there must be a point where even such a relationship as yours requires commitment. The Sag is so philosophical and righteous that your own open-mindedness was questioned and used against you. Your conversations were entertaining, but your arguments were infuriating. Luckily, the breakup will be a clean affair, as both of you are able to move on quickly. You have so much to offer the world, and so many adventures to experience.

Cancer

How many secrets can a man and woman have before they finally come to terms with the fact that they don't really know each other? You resent anyone who tries to rid you of your protective shell, and the Centaur resents anyone who clings to him. Both of you were afraid of what the other was hiding, and your attempts to find out just pushed the other farther away. You both love jokes and laughter, and that brought you together for a while—and it will help you remain friends now. The Sag was just so…pushy and self-involved. All he seemed to see in you was what you could provide for him. He never even attempted to give you the security you desperately need, and he wasn't remotely interested in taking care of you, although you did your best to care for him. There are men out there who would love your attention, who would nurture you and take care of you without teasing you and taking off at the slightest provocation.

Leo

While the two of you are highly compatible, there were certain things that drove you nuts about your Sagittarian ex. Mostly having to do with his eyes: like the way he always seemed to look down on you, or how his gaze always followed other women, or his constant searching for something else. It's true that you enjoyed his company and that he enjoyed yours. But you were so much more loyal than he was. You understand that he likes his adventures, but he rarely was willing to take you along, and a Leo simply is never treated that way. Now that you're free to find someone more adoring, don't concern yourself with what the Sag is doing. While you might remain friends, the little stabs of jealousy eventually will get old, and he'll never stop.

Virgo

While the Sag is good for laughs or conversation, a long-term relationship isn't something he has an easy time of committing to. Sure, there's the occasional Sag who meets and marries his first love and never even looks at another woman, but they are rare. And you don't like to put your heart on the line for something that simply won't work. Unlike other, less constrained signs, you have a hard time enjoying the Sag simply for what he is—a momentary companion. And you spent a lot of effort trying to make him or yourself into something neither of you are. Now that you're apart, you'll be able to see the relationship for what it was, but don't become too negative about it. There were some good things about it, and each of you learned a lot.

He'll leave you alone for the most part, and you won't exactly go trailing after him like a lost puppy. Having said that, you're more likely to find happiness with a stable sign—someone like a Taurus or a Capricorn.

Libra

There's something you can learn from a Sagittarius male. It isn't an easy lesson, but it rings with karmic repercussions. A male Centaur is hard for a Libran to resist. He presents such a challenge and is so exciting that she feels as though she *has* to be the one he settles down with. There are a couple of problems: first, he never settles down; and second, he can intuit that the Libran girl is attached, and a young Sag nearly always will take advantage of that. But the karmic ties go both ways, and he has a lesson to learn too. The breakup is fraught with demolished hopes and expectations. The Sag probably won't even treat you with the dignity and tact you've come to expect from others. However, while you keenly feel the pain of your broken heart (or just your annoyance), there are plenty of opportunities for distraction. The Sag might be a little upset when he discovers that you're the one moving on and he's the one left behind.

Scorpio

Few people have stepped all over you—without a thought about your feelings—like the Centaur has. He didn't mean to. He never means to. You're not quite sure exactly what he ever *does* mean to do. You're going to have to try not to take everything he does personally, because it doesn't really have much to do with you. That's the problem, isn't it? He never seems to think about how his actions affect others, and that's very dangerous when he's toying with the heart of a Scorpio woman. You'll let him get away with some things, even now that he isn't technically your problem anymore. But if he starts taking advantage of you or flaunting his adventures in your face, then there's a dire lesson in store for him. You have your own life to live and your own adventures to experience. You don't need an ex to constantly remind you of a past mistake.

Sagittarius

Unlike many other same-sign pairings, the two of you stand little chance of boring one another. There are far too many things to talk about and places to go, and you didn't mind having the male Sag around nearly as much as you would have with other signs. He was too free-spirited and happy to bring you down the way the others could. Now that you have broken up, there is a fairly good chance of retaining a friendship as long as both of you are respectful and neither of you has a particularly clingy Moon sign or Ascendant. You won't mind when the other moves on—because a Sag *will* move on. Even if you feel the tug of the past once in a while and wonder what might have been, there are plenty of distractions around you waiting to catch your attention.

Capricorn

You recognized qualities in the Sagittarian that you secretly wished you possessed: detachment, flamboyance, and a devil-may-care attitude. Your practicality gave you the slightest chance to tame the wayward Centaur. You knew he needed freedom and that there was always the possibility of infidelity, so you had plenty of contingency plans lined up, and you were all set to allow him a certain amount of carefully supervised freedom. You rearranged your life in order to make his more comfortable, which isn't easy for a Capricorn to do, especially when it's for someone like the Centaur who doesn't appreciate your efforts. Now that you've broken up, the Centaur will happily trot toward his next conquest, leaving you to pick up the pieces of your life. With your style and personality, one of those pieces very well might be tall, dark, and handsome.

Aquarius

You always have sensed that the issues between you and the Sagittarius ran deeper than either of you could imagine, and in a sense you're right. Both of you have some karmic obligation to each other, some lesson you must learn or teach. All things aside, though, you just might be the only female in history to get the best of a Sag. He's used to getting his way when it comes to women. He's used to being able to flit in and out of relationships, never really taking any responsibility for what he's done to his lovers. But none of that works with you. You simply don't take his half-horseshit. If he moves on a little too quickly, he'll be confused when you simply shake your head in dismissal and pity and strike up a conversation with his handsome Gemini brother. You have your own life, and you're much too important to get caught up in what your exes are doing.

Pisces

The two of you differ on a very basic level. You secretly want to be the other half of an exclusive epic love, and the Centaur would "love" everybody if he could. You are sensitive, and he is oblivious. You are tactful and polite, and he is a boorish clown. After a while, there were so many resentments between you that it's a wonder you could see each other at all. He drove you to the bottom of your ocean so many times that you felt as though you might as well stay there. You couldn't trust him, and now that he's free to do whomever he wants, all of your suspicions about his loyalty and lack of dignity have been proven true. That doesn't make you happy, but there is a certain satisfaction one gets from being right. There's already someone waiting for you. Your heart is too precious a gift to just give away, so make sure the next man deserves it.

Capricorn

The *Capricorn* Ex-Boyfriend

Dates: December 22–January 20
Planet: Saturn
Element: Cardinal earth
Representation: Goat, often depicted with the tail of a fish

Maybe it's the weight of the horns on his head that puts added pressure on his brain, or perhaps the horns just make his skull extra thick. Or maybe it's the fact that he's a cardinal sign. No matter which way you look at it, this guy is convinced that his way is the only way. New ideas don't reach him easily, and neither does pleading or reasoning. He thinks what he thinks because he thinks it, and there simply isn't much room for anything else…or anyone else. This can make him a terribly dull bully, but it also can help keep him in love with you even after a nasty breakup. Hell, it took him such a long time to admit he was in love with you (truly in love with you and not just in lust), it's only logical that it would take him a while to get over you.

There's a special kind of "push" that only the girlfriend or wife of a Capricorn can feel. It's the kind of pressure that comes from being impaled by a couple of horns, having them steer you around and force you to forsake your own choices and directions and never removing themselves from your butt until everything's over between you. Now that they finally are gone, it isn't surprising that you feel a little…freer, a little more in control, and a little less sore in the hindquarters. You now are able to follow your own inclinations and discover who you can be without Mr. Capricorn telling you what you're doing wrong, why you're doing it, why it's wrong to do it, how to stop, and how bad your life will be if you don't stop. There isn't a subject in the whole world that the Capricorn doesn't have an opinion on. And if you're still letting him control your life or even just believe that his opinion means something to you, then you'll still feel the nudge of his horns every so often.

While many astrologers claim that Mr. Capricorn never cheats, in truth, if he happens to run with a crowd that thinks cheating proves masculinity and power, he actually is more likely to cheat than most other signs, even the randy Libran and Sagittarian. Adding to the likelihood that he will cheat is his fear of making a poor decision—one that will haunt him with regret for the rest of his life. He isn't sure that you're the best he could do, but he also isn't sure that you're not the love of his life. What if you mess up all his plans? What if you were his only chance at true happiness? What if, what if, what if? It's a miracle he could decide to do anything at all. That's why he prefers to keep all of his options open, even if it means being unfaithful to his current love interest.

As an ex, his penchant for sentimentality now makes him acutely aware of what he's lost, and even if he makes a feeble attempt at getting you back, he'll never reveal just what you mean to him and how much he misses you. It's part of the tragedy of having feelings for a Capricorn. He always was so busy trying to save face and uphold his reputation that he tended to forget to show you how much he cared—although, if you were a strong asset to his reputation, he might have taken a little more notice of you than if you were merely the love of his life. Now that the two of you are apart, he's unlikely to show more emotion than he did when you were together. You might catch a whiff of bitterness somewhere down the line, or even hear a rumor that he's still in love with you ten years after the breakup, but it's rare to have more tangible material to work with—he's simply too scared of getting hurt or being wrong.

What You'll Miss

If you're the type of woman who likes to follow her husband's lead or is willing to lead him from behind the scenes (and you have the natal chart and soft hand to back it up), then the Capricorn was a good match for you and probably will be missed. He provided stability and strength. He wasn't overly emotional or clingy, and he knew what he wanted. He did value you, even if you might hear more rumors about this fact than you have actual memories to back it up. Don't doubt that he's missing you now, even if he never even tries to come back.

What You Won't Miss

The stubbornly persistent claim that he was always right. The only times this might not have been the case was when the two of you were alone without anyone to hear. Oh yeah, and the fact that you never were 100 percent certain of his love for you didn't help. It sucked. A lot. His damned reputation and ambition always came before you in any decision he had to make. You also had to deal with his admonition that he could do better, his calm assurance that it was up to you to "improve yourself" if you wanted him to stick around, and his nitpicking and griping.

How to Get Him Back
(If, for Some Reason, You Want to Know)

You always could try becoming the most powerful woman in the world. Or you could just continue supporting him and his ego, paying him constant compliments and always laughing at his jokes. You could prove how worthy an asset you are by gaining some influence in society or with the company he works for. Or you could subtly convince others to let him know what a bad decision he made by leaving you.

How to Make Sure He Stays Gone

With as little effort as he puts into getting you back, it isn't exactly hard to make sure the two of you are kaput for good. Make a good life of your own. Love yourself and be willing to hold out for someone better, maybe just even a more mature and trustworthy

Capricorn. Do what you need to do, and be successful at it. All you really need to do is turn him down once, and he won't come back again. He figures that if you want him in the future, you'll come and find him.

How Your Sign Will Handle the Situation

Aries

Both of you are highly ambitious people who often differ in your definition of success. For instance, Mr. Capricorn believed that success was simply being better than his opponents, but you felt that success was forcing your opponents to submit to your will. In essence, you have no need to achieve superiority, because your supremacy is self-evident. It's what you do with it that matters. The misunderstandings and differences of opinion won't end along with the relationship. There's a good chance that both of you are hurt, but your pride won't let the other know it. Instead, bickering and jealous insults prevail, leaving each of you even more upset. That doesn't mean you're miserable, though. He was so controlling and close-minded. He was never willing to see things your way. Now you're free to find someone who recognizes your good qualities and appreciates them rather than trying to beat them out of you.

Taurus

This is a good match, both in love and in parting. After the love affair has ended, you will either remain friends or quietly slink off in different directions, but each of you still has a certain amount of respect for the other. You understand Mr. Capricorn better than any other sign, except perhaps a female Goat. You know what to expect from him, and it's hard for him to give up the Taurus stability (truth be told, a broken heart can rattle a Goat a little, but still doesn't come close to crumbling the mountain). You aren't nearly as concerned about your reputation as he is, and if he attacks you, that is the first place he'll hit. Does he want you back? It depends on the Capricorn. Does he miss you? Of course. Even if it takes you a while to repair your broken heart, there always will be someone else to love, who will love you greatly in return.

Gemini

There's something fascinating about the Capricorn. His promises of security and stability stimulate something almost forgotten in you. But his offers come with a price: your freedom of movement and imagination. This is one man who doesn't tolerate fantasies, and he won't approve of his woman running off on adventures—especially when he isn't sure she'll be back. Any breakup between a Gemini and Capricorn will be fraught with power struggles, misunderstandings, and arguments, just as the relationship was. You had to bend over backwards to keep your relationship going, and now you'll have to work harder than you normally would to end it. But after everything has calmed down, you'll be able to rediscover yourself without his commanding presence looming over you, and knowing yourself is reward enough.

Cancer

Aside from your general compatibility, there is an underlying strain created by each of your cardinal signs. It is nearly impossible for the Goat to let others have control, and while you can pretend to be content playing second fiddle, you have an inner need to lead at least your own life. After the breakup, he'll stomp around grumbling and growling every time it looks as though you're moving on. He actually still expects you to take care of him. Now that you're free to do what you want, you'll miss the security he provided, but your newfound freedom, if enjoyed properly, will more than make up for it. There are people you've been meaning to have conversations with and men you've wanted to flirt with. You get to choose now, but don't let that frighten you. The world awaits your presence, my dear.

Leo

Goat stew, anyone? Perhaps just a roasted haunch or a foreleg to munch on? Who this man thought he was before getting into a relationship with you, and what he thought he could get away with, have now changed drastically. He admired your vibrancy, and he planned on adding you to his list of possessions: you were supposed to help bolster his reputation. And while that was flattering at first, it got old as soon as you realized that all of those suggestions he was giving you and all of his flaunting you around had nothing to do with adoring and being loyal to you but instead had everything to do with him. There isn't a Leo anywhere who will let a man get away with using her, unless she is using him too. Now that he's gone, you have more than enough of a social life to keep yourself busy. He will pout when you move on, but you'll be too busy to do more than acknowledge that he misses you.

Virgo

You understood where he was coming from. You still understand. Even though he'll never tell you that he misses you, you know he does. Wait for a decade or two, and then he'll be more than happy to reminisce about how much he loved you way back when. One problem now is that both of you are such *definite* people that you each assume the other is certain about the breakup. The two of you were good together, but neither was willing to tolerate a weakness of character in the other. And for two such judgmental people, neither of you could stand being judged. Now that you're each your own person again rather than half of a duo, there's a good chance of continued friendship or at least an amicable separation—unless one of you did something unforgivable, in which case a vast gulf separates you.

Libra

You're attracted to his strength of character and ambition. Librans, especially young ones, tend to get into relationships the same way others get into stocks: it's always best to get in on the ground floor of a probable winner. However, just because he wants to be successful doesn't mean that he will be. Capricorns have a tendency to become involved with drugs or alcohol, and get stuck there. You see, some substances give the illusion of power, and Capricorns fall in love with just about anything that gives them that feeling. That leads me to the main reason you have issues with him: his self-obsession. You can see what he's really like and what people really think of him, and it doesn't match up with his own beliefs about himself. You might have bought in to his reality for a while, but soon enough you realized the truth. He'll miss you. After all, you made him look good. But you're much better off finding someone who will love you for yourself.

Scorpio

You and Mr. Capricorn have some issues, and the breakup isn't going to be easy. He gave you loyalty and security, and you made him feel loved. The love you gave him meant a lot to him, even if he never showed you or told you so, and he's missing it now. The Capricorn is a man who finds it soothing to look back on his life and remember the people who meant a lot to him. There are a few reasons why hindsight is so comfortable for him: it doesn't require commitment, there isn't any real chance of being surprised or hurt by it, and he will be able to control any pain he feels about it. Not that you were ever supposed to know that he still thinks about you. He's afraid of the power you have over him, and he has reason to be. You represent a karmic tie, and that isn't easily dismissed. This doesn't mean you need to sit around waiting for him. You have your own life to live, and there are plenty of adventures to be had.

Sagittarius

The gilded cage he prepared for you was tempting at first. And then you noticed all the locks…and his mother sitting in the corner (Capricorns always have their mothers tucked away somewhere). He didn't understand your need for freedom, and he found your independence threatening. Don't get me wrong, there are some Capricorns out there who are intrigued by dangerous, threatening things. Intrigued? Yes. Ready to marry them? No. Not that you were ready for it either. Now that you're single again, you'll have plenty of things to occupy your mind. The Capricorn doesn't go out of his way to remind you of your relationship, and you're grateful. He'll miss you, and you'll miss him too. But there's a whole world out there waiting for you.

Capricorn

It's no secret that the two of you are alike: both of you enjoy fame, fortune, and power. However, arguments prevailed during your relationship, continuously derailing any peace you had. Both of you are so assured of the validity of your opinions that neither of you gives in easily if at all. You understood him better than any other woman has; however, you weren't quiet about the things you disliked, and he is a man who is desperate for respect. As an ex, he'd do well to remember that he can't control you the way he used to, and that it would be in his best interest to be nice and accepting if he wants to remain friends. He'll miss you greatly, and you'll miss him, for few people can get along with a Capricorn as well as another Capricorn. That doesn't mean you'll have trouble finding another suitor, though, because a female Capricorn nearly always is attractive.

Aquarius

Both of you would have had to be just a little bit odd (not in general, of course, but just according to your Sun signs) to have ended up together. For instance, he must not have been quite as rigid as Capricorns tend to be, and you must not have been quite as...eccentric as Water Bearers can be. No matter how you reflect your Sun sign, the relationship was fraught with misunderstandings and frustrations. Luckily, the breakup won't be that painful, because both of you will go your separate ways quietly—unless, of course, one of you has done something to hurt the other's ego or reputation. For the most part, you'll miss his self-assured personality, but you'll have fun regaining your freedom. There are far more entertaining companions out there, ones who will delight in your intellect and strength instead of being threatened by them.

Pisces

He gave you security and comfort. He provided you with shinny, sparkly, glittery material possessions…occasionally. But he was rigid and unfeeling. He was insensitive and blunt, loud and aggressive, and virtually everything that makes you want to glide to the bottom of your ocean and rest in the silence of your own dreams and thoughts. He didn't understand you. There is something between you, though, maybe remnants of an unresolved past life. Both of you are aware that something must be learned or sacrificed here: this feeling of obligation and mystery is what drew you together and also what eventually tore you apart. Now that you've broken up, he'll be sure to leave you some dignity, as long as you let him have his. The separation is so quiet and final, it makes it hurt worse. Don't worry, though. There are other mysterious men out there waiting to enjoy your light touch and fantasies.

Aquarius

The *Aquarius* Ex-Boyfriend

Dates: January 21–February 19
Planet: Uranus
Element: Fixed air
Representation: Water Bearer

Ah, the delightful Water Bearer. No other sign out there is served quite as many restraining orders as this gallant chap, and no other sign is so deserving of them. What an incredibly… powerful…specimen of the male ego. He's so…awe-inspiring in his ability to get under people's skin and claim titles and talents that he hasn't earned and doesn't really possess. And his heroic attempts at appearing genuine and humble can leave a woman feeling weak-kneed with a sudden wave of nausea. He is definitely a unique man, and worthy of your contempt. I think I'll have some trophies made so that all of us meek little women can give them to the superior male Aquarians in thanks for their…um…just being themselves—a marvelous deed. Anyone else need some Valium? If you've been with an Aquarius for any length of time, then you're probably looking more toward a full frontal lobotomy. But don't lose hope yet! You've survived the relationship, and now you're free to pursue other, better men (and contrary to what you've been told by this all-knowing guy, there *are* better men out there).

Dating or marrying an Aquarius has certain consequences. He's highly ambitious, so he's likely to succeed with *something* in his life. However, he's also willing to use you and your money to succeed and then drop you immediately. He isn't exactly heartless; he's just more in love with himself than with anything else in the universe. He hungers after power and control, he wants to be looked up to and admired, and he strives for respect. All of his many demands can be considered overcompensation for a rather short…um…attention span. Deep inside, he's afraid of power because he doubts if he can keep it, and he's afraid of strength because it might be challenged and he might lose it. Most of all, he's terrified of failure.

Even the best Aquarians have their quirks, and to be fair, the rest of the zodiac does too. Aquarians just tend to be a little less comprehensible than the average sign. They are highly active mentally. They'd actually prefer to be thought of as intellectual, but they tend to lack a certain originality. And *mental* doesn't necessarily mean *intelligent* either. Just because a man thinks a lot doesn't mean he's capable of formulating a new theory on quantum physics or that he has an intelligent way of thinking, let alone intelligent thoughts. In order to make up for this lack of smarts, Aquarians tend to memorize things—quotes, stories, philosophical theories, magic spells, and so on. Anything and everything that will help them gain influence or prestige. But do they really know what any of it means? Who knows?

As an ex, his pride either is hurt already or is in jeopardy of being hurt. (Whether there's a real threat to his ego is irrelevant. You've become a loose end, and he's always paranoid about loose ends.) Because Mr. Perfect Aquarian is built of hydrogen, oxygen, and egoium atoms, anything that affects his pride affects *everything*. So you can expect him to be very careful around you. Careful, but not nice or pleasant—especially if you've done something foolish enough to make him think you don't want him back. He'll spread rumors, come by your house in the middle of the night, lie, sleep with your mother if he gets the chance, etc. He wants to leave you isolated, and he insists that you pine over him. This is one man who'll never forget you, and he'll use you as a way to incite negative feelings in his current lovers—jealousy, pity, sympathy, anger. He may disappear for years only to show up on your doorstep with a police escort because he was found prowling in your bushes.

What You'll Miss

His unpredictability could make life interesting. His love of conversation helped him acquire many acquaintances and a lot of information about a variety of topics. He could be a staunch supporter, and loyal to his lover. When he wanted to, he could be quite charming as well. If you believed he was as powerful as he claimed to be at the onset of your lovely affair—and if you didn't stick around long enough to find out differently—then you probably enjoyed his confidence and strength.

What You Won't Miss

His love of hearing himself speak became embarrassing. Although he loved being important, he was rarely aware enough of the situation to understand how he really was coming across.

He supported you only when it was convenient and beneficial, and his charm was a way to manipulate people rather than encourage honest friendship. He never had friends, but only connections he could network with to gain influence or to help pressure someone into doing what he wanted them to do.

How to Get Him Back
(If, for Some Reason, You Want to Know)

Prove your importance, and then make it known that you would like a second try. Don't fawn or beg, as he will view you as weak. Stomp on all of your competition and win back his admiration while letting him know that you're not very concerned about whether he comes back to you. Be aware that he'll try out a few girls before he's ready to return, but don't hold it against him. Spend some time with one of his many rivals, someone who threatens him, but never do anything to compromise your reputation or his.

How to Make Sure He Stays Gone

Don't let him think there's a possibility he could come back. It won't make him happy, especially when you move on, but it'll be necessary because he's one man you don't want to string along. Be ready for him to do something crazy or to start spreading rumors, but stand your ground.

How Your Sign Will Handle the Situation

Aries

A tough situation. You see, the Aquarian man has a little…no, make that a large…ego, and you just don't seem to be taking care of it the way you should. According to him, thou shalt not embarrass him in public, thou shalt not be happy without him, and thou shalt not move on before he has. And damn it, you just don't seem to play by his rules! Well, *duh*. Okay, when you first got together, you might have catered to him a little. Secretly, all Aries women like to play at being outwardly submissive, at least for a while, but it gets old quickly. However, the Aquarius is upset about the whole thing. He needs to feel superior, and you're not the type to let him, so now he feels the need to prove it to you. Just move on, and don't look back at the carnage behind you. Trust yourself, trust in what you want, and don't settle for less.

Taurus

You supported him throughout, and it troubles you to think that someone might take advantage of your help. If anyone is likely to ignore the sincerity behind a Taurus woman's care, it's an Aquarian man. He took everything you offered as if it were something he deserved, and he rarely bothered to give you anything in return. Now that you've broken up, he'll still expect all the privileges he had when you were a couple, but he hasn't taken into account the firm resolve with which the Taurus can put down her foot. When you've had enough, you've had enough. You probably have to rebuild yourself a bit, because this man constantly tore you down, but it will be worth it. You need to judge for yourself whether it's a good idea to keep him as a friend. A broken heart takes time to heal.

Gemini

Few people can annoy an Aquarius like a Gemini can. He's jealous of your ease in social situations and your apparently unshakable self-confidence. He's threatened by the number of friends you have, and how his insults and rumors don't seem to shake you or them. When you were together, the two of you could talk for hours about anything. You got along all right on the surface, but the deeper issues gave you trouble. You're change-able, and the Aquarius works better in a world where he is the only one who changes. As an ex, he'll have trouble pinning you down, and eventually he'll have to accept the fact that you'll move on and leave him behind and that you might be perfectly okay if you never see or speak with him again. (He also needs to realize that he'll be okay too.) You'll be fine. You always are.

Cancer

You showed him a new way to look at the world, one that he'd never considered before, and the two of you were quickly trans-ported to another, more romantic world than the one most of us live in. However, once he memorized the new universe, he claimed it as his own—the way he usually does—and left you a little behind. He loved the way you took care of him, and he didn't mind your remoteness or need for mental privacy as much as some other men have. The major problem came when he tried to pretend he was a cardinal sign. You see, you have a natural tendency to lead, and as a fixed sign he has a tendency to resist being led. He felt threatened and insecure, and in response promptly started taking you for granted. Now that you're free again, you can find a man who'll respect you, and chances are you won't have to look far.

Leo

When the two of you were together, you were very together. Everything fit, you agreed on so much, you loved and adored each other, and the world was sunny and the air fresh. But. On the other hand. When you two were off—and you didn't need a breakup to be off—you couldn't stand anything about each other. You hated everything to do with him, and he couldn't stand to be within ten feet of you. The relationship was like a roller coaster. The one thing that drew you together, and ultimately tore you apart, was the desperate need each of you has for social status. Now that you're broken up, things could get ugly. Both of you are highly sensitive and very reactive to real and imagined slights. If you just remember that he isn't important anymore and that whatever he does will blow over in time, you'll be able to get on with your life more smoothly.

Virgo

Rarely does a Virgin experience a breakup that she didn't instigate. Even if you didn't openly end this one, you knew it was coming. You are so in control of your life (a little too in control, if you know what I mean), your every move is planned out and thought over. The Aquarius probably benefited greatly from your presence, even though he balked and bitched about your opinions; and in turn, he taught you to be a little less rigid. There isn't much he can do to you now, and you're a much bigger threat than he's used to dealing with. You see through him, whereas he doesn't quite understand you, which makes it even harder for him to pin you down. You can confront him with things that he won't admit to himself in his deepest depressions—if you cared enough to do it. There are more important things you could be doing, and you've never been anything if not practical.

Libra

It's strange how this man slipped into your life. It's almost as if he did it when you weren't looking, and through his own sheer will. Creepy. Even though you are the cardinal sign, he was adamant about being the leader, and you knew that if you wanted to stay with him you'd have to at least pretend to be his subordinate. But while you're a good actress, the game got old, and you eventually found a way to gain some type of control. After the breakup, the Aquarius will alternate between brooding and begging you to come back. He's a better stalker than Mr. Scorpio because the Aquarius is methodical and rational, rarely getting caught. He's threatened by your charm and the ease with which you move on.

Scorpio

It's hard to predict what will happen with this breakup. Both of you can be explosive, paranoid people. But then, both of you are likely to surprise everyone by calmly moving on without hesitation. The cool rationality with which the Water Bearer views everything left you feeling invalidated and alone. He didn't understand your passions or your fears, and you never felt completely comfortable with him. Once he lost your respect, you enjoyed taunting him into expressions of anger, and he would retaliate by inciting your jealousy. It was a vicious cycle. Now that you're free of his constant judgments and manipulations, you can find someone who will help you build the type of relationship you desire—one based on emotional support, trust, love, and respect.

Sagittarius

You are a fun friend and an exciting lover, and are very low maintenance in a relationship. You know how to appreciate a joke and how to accept someone for who he is. However, you're also very intuitive, and you didn't buy the Aquarian's assertion that he was all-knowing and all-powerful. At first you dealt with it tactfully, but eventually you let him know what you really thought. He knew he couldn't fool you through intimidation or argumentation, and it threatened him. There's a karmic tie between you, a puzzle that both of you may enjoy figuring out. (After all, you both love riddles.) Hopefully he's learned by now that it's easier to be your friend than your enemy, and that you're open to having him as either. As for you, you'll quickly move on. You have no trouble being nice to your exes, and they rarely get the upper hand over you.

Capricorn

Almost from the start, you had a lot of trouble respecting the Aquarian. You understand the urge to talk big, but his lies were so transparent, not to mention embarrassing, and you couldn't fathom why he'd keep it up. The fact that he intuited your lack of respect and tried to manipulate and intimidate you didn't help either. You need to feel secure before you can pledge your heart to a man, but there was something about Mr. Water Bearer that made you hesitate more than usual. Now that he's your ex, you'll be able to figure out what that something was (like his mental instability, for example). He won't be able to scare you the way he does other signs, because your life is simply too solid for his hot air to disturb.

Aquarius

First off, congrats if you stuck around long enough to get to this part of the chapter. In all honesty, the female Aquarian tends to be a bit more grounded—and less psycho—than her male counterpart. The two of you probably got along well, each of you admiring the other's intelligence and opinions. Your arguments resembled college debates more than heavily emotional affairs. It was the leadership thing that might have started the problems, or maybe it was your mutual stubbornness. Now that you've parted, you'll need to work extra hard to maintain some respect for each other, as that is the only way to calm the storm. There's a chance for great friendship if each of you handles the separation with tact.

Pisces

Okay, a woman can take only so much belittling before she starts to lose sight of herself (or else leaves the man who's doing it), and although you can tolerate more than most, the Aquarius's lack of respect challenges even you. He loves your femininity and your apparent submissiveness, but he quickly took you for granted. Unfortunately, he won't realize how much this hurts you until you've already done something about it—like moving on. It seemed as though he always was trying to pressure you into a fight, and you don't like fighting. After the separation, it still feels like he's always trying to start an argument. Only now, rather than attempting to ease his boredom, he's trying to ascertain whether you still care enough about him to fight with him. He'll be surprised and hurt when you move on, but once you're through with him there will be little he can do about it.

Pisces

The *Pisces* Ex-Boyfriend

Dates: February 20–March 20
Planet: Neptune
Element: Mutable water
Representation: Two Fish chasing each other's tails

I could end this chapter right now with two words that explain everything Mr. Pisces ever has done and ever will do: "He's nuts." But, of course that would be too simple for a Pisces and too much to the point. On the surface, this man appears to be the epitome of sweetness; he's got sob stories on every subject, could make a pro wrestler cry with his accounts of love gone wrong (the fault of all those vicious women who have purposely duped him over the years with lies about commitment, good living, and plenty of sex), and is willing to stoop so low to get what he wants that his breath reeks of soil and night crawlers. He's not completely oblivious to the fact that he manipulates others; he just doesn't understand that he doesn't have to play games in order to get what he wants, that sometimes he can just ask.

Of course, asking for what he wants becomes a little complicated by his inability to openly go after what he wants just because he wants it. Instead, he needs to create a story to convince everyone else that he deserves to have something so that they can provide the energy and momentum he needs to go after it. It's not that he's impotent without public approval; he just finds it easier to deflect any blame or guilt over his actions if he can prove that others pushed him into doing it. By the way, this is how he escapes being accountable for any real wrongdoing after a relationship, and how he somehow has managed to turn even your own mom against you. He will play the role of the guilt-ridden hero who selflessly tried everything to make the relationship work, and he even will pretend to take accountability for just enough of the mistakes to convince people that he's being selflessly honest about his role in the breakup.

Oftentimes Pisces never learn how to handle disappointment or deal with negative emotions or consequences, and this plays out horrifically in their adult lives: you will never find another sign as confused as the Pisces. The poor things know that something is wrong, but can never seem to figure out what it is, let alone how to fix it—that's also why Pisces is the sign of the perpetual therapy patient. You probably watched him jump around from friend to friend, and from psychiatrist to support group, searching for a way to reconcile the conflicts between his inner self and the world around him and leaving a trail of disappointments and empty promises in his wake. It slowly dawned on you that you were just another step he felt he needed to take in order to understand himself, and that now he's moving on to the next experiment. Despite his reputation as the Mother Teresa of the zodiac, he's strangely oblivious to any emotions, desires, or needs outside of his own. He simply doesn't seem to care about what you're feeling, unless it in some way affects his ability to get what he wants.

During the relationship, you had to hold his itty-bitty hand through many of his periods of doubt and depression, reassuring him that he *is* good enough, damn it, and fearing that if he didn't find the comfort he needed in you, he'd be more than willing to look for it elsewhere. Now that you've broken up, you're still expected to take care of him, and anything you do that isn't in his best interest is seen as a direct attempt to hurt him. He will be ready for you to move on only once he has done so; however, anything that happens now will validate him in some way: if you hurt him, it proves he is the victim; if you beg him to return, he must be someone worth missing. He can make up any story to prove whatever point he wants to. It's important to know that he is the creator of his world, not a victim of it.

What You'll Miss

His sweetness and his sensitivity to your moods and desires. He always tried to get you what you wanted, and he was desperate to stay on your good side. He is fair about any subject that doesn't involve him, and he enjoys a variety of hobbies. He's absolutely wonderful for any woman looking to practice her nurturing. He makes a good shoulder to cry on, if you can ignore his hand on the back of your head trying to force it to his crotch.

What You Won't Miss

His manipulations, pity parties, and absolute assurance that if something went wrong, it was someone else's fault (and yet he found a way to appear completely guilt-ridden while blaming anyone handy). Then there was the ease with which he could fall into another woman's bed, and the difficulty he seemed to have staying out of it. According to him, everything that went wrong in your relationship was your fault—except a few choice things he's willing to take responsibility for to make himself look better and more honorable.

How to Get Him Back
(If, for Some Reason, You Want to Know)

There's a good way and a bad way. The good way: make sure he realizes he has the tools to make up his own mind (some Pisces *are* raised rather well, and they have much fewer issues than others of their sign). Let him know exactly how you feel and what you think of the situation, and then ask him if he's willing to make some compromises. If he loves you, and if you're willing to communicate, then everything should go well. The bad way: beg him, tell him that you can't live without him and that he simply needs to come home, basically guilt-trip him. I warn you, though, if you go after him the bad way, he won't stick around long.

How to Make Sure He Stays Gone

This man likes to leave and come back so often that all you have to do is tell him to go away and then ignore his guilt-tripping and crying. "Blah. Blah. Blah. Mistake. Blah. Your fault. Yadda yadda. Take me back. Blah. Bullshit promises." And once he's gone, ignore everything he does to hurt you: rumors, blaming, sleeping with your best friend, etc.

How Your Sign Will Handle the Situation

Aries

No one puts out your fire quite like a water sign can, and the Pisces is deep ocean, darlin'. He's the most wishy-washy passive-aggressive sign there is, and I commend you for trying to forge a relationship with him. The persona he showed you in the beginning, the one you felt compelled to get close to and understand, didn't last long. Eventually you understood how changeable he is, how he never gave you the full story or completely answered any of your searching questions—and it left you feeling a little out of sorts and doubtful about the future of your affair. You love your ideals and fantasy, but even you can appreciate solid ground under your feet now and then, unlike Mr. Pisces. Now that you're free to wander to your own tune again, you'll be able to maintain friendship with him only if you learn to accept his aloofness. Most men would rather fan your passionate flames than douse them.

Taurus

The inconstancy of the Pisces, and his habit of never letting anyone into his internal world, did not make for a firm foundation on which to build a relationship, and you *love* security. At first you ignored his constantly changing ideas and his inability to get a secure hold on reality (unless, of course, he has the influence of a firmer sign in his chart), but you eventually came to realize that you couldn't trust much of what he told you. He was so passive when it came to his ambitions, so diluted in his beliefs, that you never could get a grasp on who he really was or, even more importantly, who he eventually would become. Somewhere, somehow, there is something important to learn from him, but eventually you will have had enough. There are more stable prospects out there, some of whom are even as in touch with reality as you are, waiting for a woman like you to come along.

Gemini

His constant fear that he couldn't hold on to you turned him into a nagging, jealous, passive-aggressive tyrant, and it even might have given him an excuse to cheat on you (after all, he couldn't control whether or not you were cheating on him, and this was his bizarre way of taking more control of a situation that was causing him so much grief). If either of you was depressed, the other inevitably became so in response, and if one of you had a substance abuse problem, the other one may have developed an addiction too. Eventually both of you were caught in an argument over who's fault everything was, and it was you who usually took the blame, because the Pisces was so guilt-ridden himself that he simply couldn't be blamed for anything else. You feel an air of immense freedom, with only a twinge of loss, now that you're no longer with him. You've forgotten all the adventures you used to have, and you're itching to go on some new ones.

Cancer

The two of you were—are—remarkably in sync. The things that usually bother other signs about the Pisces didn't really bug you. Both of you are perfectly content to live in a separate world from the rest of us, but your worlds didn't always coincide. The major problem stemmed from your need for security and his inability to offer much of it. He never is truly successful at work, even if his ambitions are high, and there isn't a Pisces out there who can promise absolute fidelity, just like there aren't many Cancer women willing to settle for less than just that. The breakup hurt each of you deeply, almost as if a huge chunk of your body was wrenched away. There might have been a good reason for your relationship to end—like infidelity or bankruptcy—and there always will be other chances for true love.

Leo

Things started out well, until you each began to rack up resentments. Neither of you is absolutely open about your innermost feelings, because neither of you trusts people easily and both of you are rulers of your own worlds. The silences stretched on as emotions raged, and conversations that were desperately needed were put off too long. In a way you were perfect together: the Pisces is the perfect subject, outwardly obliging and a challenge to get inside of; and you are the perfect ruler, both warm and protective. Without the Pisces to hold you back with his pouting and "you're hurting my feelings" glares, you'll be able to find a better companion, one who will challenge you and soothe you, one whom you can cuddle without the fear that all you have of him is his body. One who will give you his heart too.

Virgo

Although Mr. Pisces provided you with the loving, tender support you've always (somewhat secretly) looked for from a man, he simply was too emotional and wimpy for you. He didn't know where he was going in life. Financial success was a fun daydream but nothing he was willing to work for, and *monogamy* didn't fit in his personal dictionary. He was willing to live with your rules, and strove to make the changes you suggested, but you want a man who can think for himself and meet you on your level—something that Mr. Pisces didn't know how to do. Manipulation is his life: it's something he's done since he was little, and in fact one could consider it his one true talent. When looking for your next partner, wouldn't it be better to stick to your standards for once rather than settling for a fixer-upper? You deserve it.

Libra

The two of you will get along well after the breakup simply because you are tactful and can see through all of his tricks. Unless you haven't had much experience with love (most Librans have had plenty of experience by age six), you didn't buy all of his far-out promises, so you aren't incredibly disappointed now. The idea of marrying him was nice to toy around with, but actually forming a lasting commitment till death do us part made you contemplate murder. During your relationship, the two of you had a lot in common and enjoyed each other's company. Both of you can be deeply sensitive to your environment, and you knew how to provide the ego reinforcement Mr. Pisces needs.

Scorpio

While you are a highly compatible pair, there was plenty of room for disaster. Both of you are very emotional; however, you are more possessive than Mr. Pisces. He never understood your fear that he'd cheat on you—even though it's something he was more than capable of doing—or your need for reassurance that he wouldn't. He has more than a slight need for reassurance himself, which you were very good at giving him as long as the relationship was secure. After the breakup, you'll be hurt and upset.

Both of you will. It's hard to find someone so compatible, who understands you so well, and then deal with his new, maybe even lesser, position in your life. But you'll be fine. It'll just take some time.

Sagittarius

Admittedly, you enjoy your adventures and prefer a life of excitement, but even you understand the pleasure of stability with someone you love. The Pisces was just so *weird*. And *emotional*. And *emotionally manipulative*. His manipulative tactics exhausted you and left you with more than a little resentment. He had so many quirks to maneuver around, so many strange obstacles to overcome. He was a fun, charming companion, but also a dangerous and unpredictable adversary. As an ex, he'll vacillate between pretending never to have known you and claiming that he was the love of your life. But despite all appearances and troubles, something drew you together, and you'll never forget one another. Moving on won't be difficult; you're too quick to find the good and attractive in others.

Capricorn

A Goat can love a Fish, but where would they make their home? You enjoy solid ground under your feet, whereas a Pisces would surely suffocate if forced to live for too long outside of his fantasy world—even though he is desperate for the security you provided. His interpretation of reality initially gave you a break from your overly structured life, but as soon as you realized that it was the way he lived his life, the charm faded. You just can't understand, or respect, someone who deals with every problem by escaping from it into fantasy. As for Mr. Pisces, he admired your ability to take on every challenge, but when the relationship hinged on forcing him to accept the real world, he wished you would just leave him alone. As an ex, he'll quietly retreat into the background and let you live the life you want to. He's too afraid to interfere, and too pessimistic you push himself past the fear.

Aquarius

It is perhaps this relationship that gives meaning to your title, the Water Bearer…or perhaps Barer. At your best, the two of you were strangely compatible: Mr. Pisces benefited from your intellectual conversation and rationality, and you needed his compassion and support. Even now that the romantic relationship has ended, you are capable of maintaining a close friendship if you want to. Of course, his emotionality got under your skin. You had trouble sympathizing with his self-created problems, and you couldn't understand his reluctance to handle obstacles. He held you hostage emotionally and refused to be held accountable for anything he'd done. You grew tired of the power struggles and of shouldering most of the responsibility. Moving on won't be difficult.

Pisces

The two of you were too passive to last for long. Each of you needed more direction than the other could provide. Both of you may have strived to make the other happy, or you may have escaped into separate fantasy worlds, ignoring the relationship you had and letting it go down the drain along with the bath water. There's no telling exactly what will happen between you, and few know the truth of what occurred before the breakup. I can almost guarantee that he won't forget you, and that there will be times when you will miss him dearly. The two of you are so alike that it will be hard to maintain any animosity. You will move on, and so will he, but there always will be a special place in your heart for memories of him—once the pain wears off.

About the Author

Rowan Davis lives in Texas with her incredibly tolerant husband and even more tolerant horses, without each of whom she would be a hundredth of the woman she is today.